10 COMMON MISTAKES FINANCIAL ADVISORS MAKE & SIMPLE IDEAS TO AVOID THEM

10 COMMON MISTAKES FINANCIAL ADVISORS MAKE & SIMPLE IDEAS TO AVOID THEM

How to Create Happy, Loyal Clients

HOWARD LASHNER

The material contained herein is for informational purposes only and the opinions and statements are solely those of the author, Howard Lashner. The ideas contained in this book are guidelines, ideas and best practices utilized by Mr. Lashner over the course of his financial services career. This material should not be construed as an offer to sell or a solicitation to buy any insurance or securities product. Following the guidance contained in this book does not guarantee financial professionals will achieve any level of success in their business.

Copyright © 2018 Howard Lashner

All rights reserved. No part of this book may be used or reproduced in any manner whatsoever without written permission, except in the case of brief quotations in critical articles and reviews. For more information, contact Howard Lashner at Howard@lashner.biz or call (267) 784-4420.

Howard Lashner asserts his moral right to be identified as the author of this book.

This book is dedicated to all of the people who have helped, mentored and influenced my thinking and approach to helping clients.

Contents

A Few Thoughts to Start 3

Chapter 1
Common Mistake:
Too Much Jargon, Not Enough Clarity

Best Practice:
Keep Your Language and Processes Clear and Simple 7

Chapter 2
Common Mistake:
Building a Client Relationship on Selling a Commodity

Simple Idea:
Build a Client Relationship on Trust 23

Chapter 3
Common Mistake:
Trying to Sell or Implement **Your** *Plan Right from the Start*

Simple Idea:
Learn Client Concerns and What They Want and Need—Then Deliver! 37

Chapter 4
Common Mistake:
Trying to Do It All by Yourself

Simple Idea:
Develop an Administrative Staff—Even If It's One Person 47

Chapter 5
Common Mistake:
Relying Too Heavily on High Tech Instead of High Touch

Simple Idea:
More Personalization, Less Automation 65

Chapter 6
Common Mistake:
Not Properly Setting the Stage for References and Introductions

Simple Idea:
Make Yourself Referable 75

Chapter 7
Common Mistake:
Not Doing Regular Customer Follow-Up

Simple Idea:
Create a Systematic Client Follow-Up Relationship 83

Chapter 8
Common Mistake:
To Get Big, Focus on the Big Things

Simple Idea:
Never Be Too Big to Do the Little Things 91

Chapter 9
Common Mistake:
Bringing Up Politics with Clients

Simple Idea:
Talk Economics, Avoid Politics 95

Chapter 10
Common Mistake:
Compounding Mistakes by Not Handling Them Properly

Simple Idea:
Admit, Learn, Don't Repeat 97

A Few Thoughts to Close 107

Acknowledgments 110

About the Author 111

10 COMMON MISTAKES FINANCIAL ADVISORS MAKE & SIMPLE IDEAS TO AVOID THEM

> *Even if you are on the right track you'll get run over if you just sit there.*
> —Will Rogers

A Few Thoughts to Start

As financial advisors, we operate in a dynamic, ever-changing investment world. New products, new programs, and new regulations impact the markets and our business. It is essential that we stay up to date and informed and that we build a relationship of trust with existing and potential clients.

One thing seems to always remain the same: Many potential clients have fears about working with financial advisors. They are intimidated by the idea. They are not sure whom to trust with their life savings. Some don't think they have enough money to invest, so, they don't think a professional would help them much; or they think they can't afford to use a financial advisor. In a word, many potential clients feel overwhelmed.

Investment companies understand these fears, and some have built their advertising campaigns around the gap between client perceptions and the reality of what their investment professionals can do for them.

As a financial advisor, do you know what you personally can do to close the gap, alleviate fears, and build trust with your client? This book is designed to help you discover actions you can take to create happy clients and lasting relationships with them.

For more than two decades I have had the privilege of traveling around the country meeting with and speaking to groups of my fellow financial advisors. In these professional gatherings I've been struck by the fact that what many advisors—both newly licensed and experienced veterans—consider to be their standard operating procedures are what I consider to be missed opportunities to build better, longer-lasting client relationships.

I began jotting down the most common mistakes and missed opportunities I encountered. I then thought about the successful people I have met along the way whose suggestions and perspectives have had a big impact on my career. I asked myself several questions: How did they work with clients? Why were those clients loyal? What persuaded their clients to feel comfortable enough to introduce them to family, friends, and coworkers?

I next thought about how I have built upon what I learned from others to create my own successful business. I also took an honest look at how I continue to make some easily remedied mistakes as if they were ingrained habits.

Looking for ways to improve my own skills, as well as sharing what I have learned along the way, is the genesis of this book.

I compiled ten common mistakes and the simple, commonsense solutions to overcome them. My selections were based on both eliminating mistakes that keep financial advisors from delivering to their clients the highest-level experience possible and those mistakes that impede financial advisors in expanding their business and client roster. The result is my philosophy on how to work with clients, and a plan of action that you can implement.

My goal is to see things from the client perspective in ways that help them become debt free, financially independent, and properly protected. It is a true honor to have clients entrust me with a large portion of their net worth and savings.

Each mistake and its best-practice remedy are covered in a separate chapter. I use real-world client experiences, as well as several of my own, to illustrate specific issues and points. I'm sure many of you have run into similar situations. I'm also sure you'll see how simple changes can have positive impacts.

One note about terminology: You'll notice that throughout this book I use the title *financial advisor*. I do so because it is the title most commonly used by clients, FINRA, the SEC and the Department of Labor. Of course, there are numerous other professional designations for the men and women who provide financial services. These include:

- Registered Rep
- Investment Advisor Representative
- Investment Advisor
- Registered Investment Advisor
- Financial Planner
- Certified Financial Planner
- Personal Financial Specialist
- Chartered Financial Analyst
- Chartered Financial Consultant

I am licensed as a Registered Rep and Investment Advisor Representative. No matter what your title or professional designation may be, I hope you gain a better understanding of how to minimize mistakes and improve the overall client experience.

> *Progress is man's ability to complicate simplicity.*
> —Thor Heyerdahl

CHAPTER 1

Common Mistake:
Too Much Jargon, Not Enough Clarity

Best Practice:
Keep Your Language and Processes Clear and Simple

One very common mistake financial advisors make that frequently frustrates clients is, they don't keep it simple.

Many financial advisors complicate their client discussions with industry jargon, undefined terms, and information that soars over the listener's head. Why do so many of us do this? I believe we do it out of insecurity—we want to appear not only smart but also invaluable. Financial markets can be complicated. Clients are entrusting us with their life savings, or at least a significant portion of it. We want to prove that we are smart, are worth doing business with, and that their investments are in good hands.

But when financial advisors overuse jargon or don't take the time to explain terms, it is the client who becomes insecure. When hearing financial jargon pour out of a financial advisor's mouth, all the client can concentrate on is defining an unfamiliar term in their head while missing important details that follow. Clients don't want to become experts in our field. They don't want to know what APY or LTV[*] stand for. They hire us because we are the experts. If we don't "translate" jargon into everyday English, they are left wondering if they are making the right decision in working with us.

In my years in helping clients as a financial advisor, I have learned the value of keeping it simple. That doesn't mean talking down to clients. On the contrary, it means presenting information in a clear, concise way and spending the time to make sure they understand what I am telling them. I strive to do this every single time with every single client. When clients tell me that this is their first time working with a financial professional where they truly understand what is being said, that is one of the highest compliments I can be paid.

One way I keep in mind to watch my jargon is to remember my experiences as a customer. After all, every one of us is a client or customer of another business or service. Since we likely don't deal with that business or service every day, jargon that is second nature to a representative may sound like a foreign language to you.

Let me share an experience I had with a customer-service representative. I'm confident many of you can relate.

I purchased a treadmill with an extended warranty. During the warranty period the motor died. I called the store where I purchased the treadmill. They said I had to call the manufacturer. I called the manufacturer. They said I had to call the warranty company. I was already frustrated, and I hadn't even spoken to anyone yet about resolving my problem.

I called the warranty company and was placed on hold for thirty minutes. When I finally reached a representative, he said that he would write up and submit the ticket to see if the motor repair was under warranty. He also said that I would have to call back to follow up. The representative was placing responsibility back on my shoulders, which compounded my frustration.

---

[*] APY—Annual Percentage Yield; LTV—Loan to Value.

Several days later I called again, and I was again on hold for approximately thirty minutes. At last a representative answered. Here is how the conversation went:

Howard: I'm calling to find out if my motor repair is still under warranty.

> *Representative:* I see that the ticket has been written up.

Howard: Okay. Do I have to pay for a service call to install the motor?

> *Representative:* Sir, I told you, the ticket has been written up. It's been submitted.

Howard: Does that mean I don't have to pay for a service call?

> *Representative:* Sir, I'm going to say this one more time, the ticket has been written up and submitted.

His voice was tinged with annoyance. He talked to me like I was the stupidest person in the world and, I still had no idea what he was telling me. I pressed on.

Howard: I'm sorry. I don't understand what that means. I'm asking a simple yes or no question. Do I have to pay for the service call?

> *Representative:* Sir, if you'll stop talking and just listen—I'm going to say this one more time. The ticket has been submitted.

Howard: And I'm going to say this one more time—I don't know what "the ticket has been submitted" means! Does it mean I don't have to pay? I do have to pay? What are you telling me?

Representative: It's been handled. You don't have to pay.

To the representative, "the ticket has been submitted" is in-house jargon meaning that the item is under warranty and service is covered. To me, it was five random words that did not answer my direct question.

This may seem like an extreme example—unfortunately it was all too real—but it not only shows how frustrating jargon can be to a client, it doesn't always answer the question. Think about the terms you use that are second nature to you but may be meaningless or confusing to your clients.

How can you keep it simple?

Let's start by looking at a challenge we face with clients. Are you familiar with the expression "A little knowledge is a dangerous thing?"

It's likely that every client has heard of bonds, and if asked, would say they know what they are. Here are some answers clients gave when asked what a bond is:

- It's like a stock, but more conservative.

- It's something you give to children to save for college.

- A bond pays interest.

- They are low risk.*

---

* All bonds carry some degree of risk, such as those related to principle, interest rate and purchasing power.

These answers have elements of truth to them, but they don't tell the whole story, nor do they take into account the many different types of bonds available, like corporate bonds, treasury bonds, and municipal bonds, along with many variations of bond funds. Most clients don't want to appear financially unsophisticated, so, when the topic of bonds comes up, they'll often nod and say okay without asking questions. They have a little knowledge and they think that is good enough. Don't let "good enough" be good enough for your clients.

Because they may not fully understand the risks associated with bonds, we must educate our clients so that we can best manage their expectations.

One way to educate and keep it simple is by letting clients know what a financial term means—in this case, *bond*—and exactly what you mean when you use the term—as in, for example, a *corporate bond*.

Here is the definition of the word *bond*, according to Investopedia.com:

> A bond is a debt instrument in which an investor loans money to an entity (typically corporate or governmental), which borrows the funds for a defined period of time at a variable or fixed interest rate. Owners of bonds are debt holders, or creditors, of the issuer.

That is a pretty straightforward definition. But *debt instrument, entity, defined period of time*—those are lackluster, dry descriptions that likely would still be confusing to clients and perhaps raise questions.

How can you take information and make it simple and easily understood for clients? I like a technique called *storyselling*—telling a simple story that makes it easy for clients to relate to and understand your terminology. My experience with the warranty representative is an example of storyselling around confusing jargon.

Now let's take a look at two storyselling examples of how to inform and educate your clients about bonds in general and about the risks involved in including them in an investment portfolio.

Storyselling:
Henry and Ruth Want to Know More about Corporate Bonds

Henry and Ruth own corporate bonds through some of their 401(k) mutual-fund holdings, but don't fully understand bonds and want to learn more about them. I would storysell as follows:

> Henry and Ruth, you have $10,000 in your savings account at your bank. It yields 1 percent interest. It's a safe place for your money, but at 1 percent your money is not working very hard for you. Your next-door neighbor Rob is a successful entrepreneur. Rob goes to your bank to get a $10,000 loan. The bank offers it to him at 10 percent interest. Because he's a good entrepreneur, Rob has a better idea. He comes to you and says, "Take your $10,000 out of the 1 percent savings account and lend it to me for two years. I will pay you 6 percent interest." You make more; Rob pays less. The middleman—the bank—is eliminated. But how do you know Rob's company can repay the loan? He gives you an I.O.U.
>
> Essentially, a bond certificate is an I.O.U., but instead of being issued by an individual it is issued—or sold—by a corporation, municipality or country.

Now armed with more knowledge, Henry and Ruth have one question: "Are there risks involved with bonds?"

Here is a storyselling way to answer their question:

> Let's say you have a 10-year, $10,000 bond that pays 3 percent interest. After the first year you decide you need your money. You call your neighbor Rob, tell him that you have a 3 percent

bond, and ask if he would like to buy it from you. Rob says he can get 5 percent interest on his $10,000 from the bank. You say, "Okay, I'll give it to you for $9,000." That's called selling at a discount. The rates went up; you lost money.

On the other hand, let's say you call Rob and make the 3 percent offer, and now he says, "Your offer of 3 percent is amazing, I'm only getting 1 percent at the bank. Of course I'll give you $10,000." Now the bond is more valuable, so you tell Rob, "I want $11,000 for it." That's called selling at a premium.

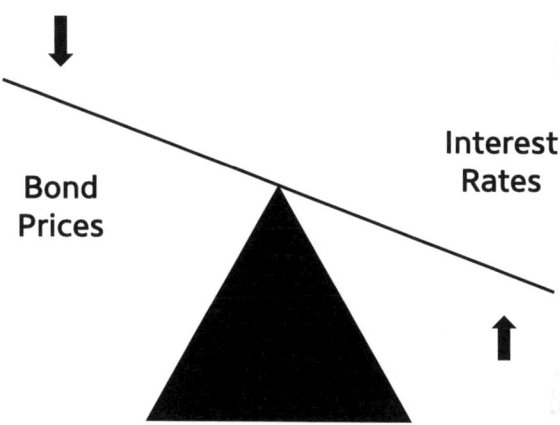

Of course, this is an oversimplification, but in my experience clients will clearly understand that when rates go up, their bond becomes less valuable; when rates go down, the bonds are more valuable.

Storyselling:
Should Janet Pay Off Her Mortgage?

The storyselling technique is applicable to any financial product or situation. Let me give you another example, this time about whether or not a client should pay off her mortgage.

You explain to Janet that she is in a position to pay off her mortgage, yet Janet prefers to continue making payments because she believes she needs the tax deduction.

There are some situations where that may be the case, but it's not the case for Janet. She would be better off being debt free. How, as Janet's financial advisor, do you storysell that a tax deduction is not necessarily financially desirable?

> *Financial Advisor:* Janet, let's play a game. Let's assume you are in the 22 percent tax bracket. If I came to you and said for every dollar you give me I will give you 22 cents back, how many dollars would you want to give me?
>
> *Janet:* None. I'd be getting ripped off.
>
> *Financial Advisor:* Well, that's what happens when you pay a dollar in interest on your mortgage. If you have to pay interest, it is better to get some money back through a deduction, but it is best to pay nothing at all. Wouldn't you agree?"
>
> *Janet:* Absolutely!
>
> *Financial Advisor:* That's why it benefits you to become debt free.*

If you would like to learn more about storyselling, I highly recommend the book *Storyselling for Financial Advisors: How Top Producers Sell*, by Scott West and Mitch Anthony. They provide a number of stories to help financial advisors communicate with different types of clients.

---

* Of course, there are exceptions to every rule. However, for most people becoming debt free is a huge step towards becoming financially independent.

KEEP THE PROCESSES AND EXPERIENCE SIMPLE

Keeping it simple is not limited to how you communicate with clients. It also applies to making the process and experience as easy and simple as possible for our clients.

Let me give you an example of how making something simple makes a customer's life easier and their experience more pleasant—often without their even realizing you have done so.

I'm sure most of you have shopped on Amazon. If you have, then you have probably used its "Buy Now with 1-Click" option. It is the ultimate in shopping convenience. Jeff Bezos, founder of Amazon, committed many hours and millions of dollars to having his IT department go from the industry pervasive 2-Click system to the Amazon 1-Click system, which Amazon then registered. Why was Bezos so committed? He wanted to make the buying process as simple as possible for his customers. When told that what he wanted was nearly impossible, he insisted his team find a way.

Think about it. How long does it really take to click a mouse twice? A fraction of a second. But Jeff Bezos knew that in a competitive market you have to find the competitive edge. "Buy Now with 1-Click" became Amazon's competitive edge—and one that Bezos was willing to share. Today, companies around the world pay Amazon royalties for the use of 1-Click technology. Now, when customers shop online, they expect a 1-Click experience. An innovation that customers didn't even know they wanted has now become a customer expectation.

How can you innovate and raise your customer expectations in ways that surprise and delight them?

As financial advisors, we have many different competitors, like Robo Advisors and high-tech firms who strive to simplify the process through online services. Financial advisors offering face-to-face customer service can create a competitive edge by simplifying customer stress points. Complex, jargon-laced conversation is one stress point. So are excessive applications and paperwork.

Have any of your clients expressed frustration with receiving paperwork in the mail that is not only written in complicated legalese, but also relies on them to fill in the many blanks? Maybe you've even experienced this yourself as a client when dealing with lawyers, accountants or financial institutions. Some questions are open to interpretation and your client would like a further explanation. They call the toll-free number listed in the paperwork, are kept on hold listening to canned music for far too long, and finally get a customer representative on the line. Frequently the call-center reps have not been trained to respond to questions—especially those "off-script"—in a simple manner. Instead, they pepper your client with questions like these:

- Is this a before- or after-tax contribution?

- Which specific funds do you want to take your withdrawal from?

- What is the address of the fund company the check should be mailed to?

These are just a few of the many questions my clients have told me they find confusing.

Clients are left frazzled. Often, they ask their question in an awkward fashion and the call-center representative answers a different question altogether (*i.e.*, "your ticket has been submitted"). Misunderstandings frequently occur. The simplest tasks become frustrating and time consuming. And adding a third party that doesn't know your client's background adds unnecessary stress to the situation. More important—*it minimizes your value to your client.*

How can you easily demonstrate your value and reduce customer frustration? Have forms and paperwork completed to the best of your ability before you meet with your client. You already have your existing client's basic information: name, date of birth, job, assets and liabilities, etc. Enter this information beforehand. If any updates are needed, your client will tell you, while also being relieved that so much of this simple information they've given you before is already entered.

Loan closers exemplify the effectiveness of having paperwork prefilled before the meeting. A loan closer has two sets of documents. They review the paperwork quickly and thoroughly and the client signs one set in front of them. What could otherwise have been a one-hour meeting now only takes twenty minutes. Being prepared is the mark of a true professional.

Here are some other easy ways to demonstrate your preparedness. If your client needs to write a letter of instruction, write it for them and have them verify that the information is correct before they sign. If the letter needs to be sent, provide them with a stamped, addressed envelope. If the document needs to be notarized, arrange for a notary public to be in your office if one is not already there. Do whatever it takes to make the process more efficient and ensure its completion in a timely manner.

Does this seem like a lot of extra effort? It is—and with good reason. The best way to be valuable to your client is to keep yourself in the equation whenever possible. Set your client up for success. Make working with you a positive experience and reduce stress points as much as you can.

You are providing a service and it is your responsibility to treat your clients in ways that create loyalty and advocacy.

Chapters 4 and 5 go into detail on the importance of having the right people and processes in place and delivering a personalized experience to make your clients' lives—and your own—easier.

Storyselling:
Holding-Pattern Frustrations

Let me share a personal story with you to illustrate the importance of having the right people and processes in place.

Recently my wife and I bought a sofa from the local store of a well-known national furniture company. After it was delivered, we noticed some fabric damage. I immediately called the store to let them know. I was told that I had to call a toll-free number for customer service. I called and listened to an automated phone system with numerous choices, but none offering the chance to talk to a live person. After pushing various buttons only to be consistently returned to the initial prompt, I hung up and once again called the local store. I didn't reach the first person with whom I spoke. The person who answered asked me a few questions then put me on hold. A few minutes later she got back on the line, asked a few more questions, then asked if it was okay to put me back on hold. At this point I had invested twenty minutes of my time; an extra minute or two wouldn't make a difference in time spent—but it was making a difference in my attitude toward the store. Next, the first person I spoke to returned to the line, apologized for "the confusion" and said, "I'll schedule a fabric repair specialist to come to your house."

Although the end result was I got what I wanted, the process was frustrating and totally unnecessary. How likely do you think I'll purchase furniture at that store again or recommend the store to my friends and family? Not very likely. It would be likely, however, that I would tell friends and family about my negative experience with the store.

Now, let's replay my initial telephone call to the store and see how keeping the process simple makes a world of difference to the customer experience.

> *Howard:* My newly purchased sofa was just delivered and there is some fabric damage.
>
>> *Customer Representative:* I am so sorry Mr. Lashner. I know how frustrating that can be. Let me see what I can do to quickly take care of this for you. (Does not place me on hold) I can have a fabric repair specialist come to your house on Wednesday. Would that work for you?
>
> *Howard:* Two days from now? That would be fine. Thank you.
>
>> *Customer Representative:* And thank you for letting us know immediately so that we can handle it for you. We want you to have many happy years with your new sofa. Is there anything else I can help you with?
>
> *Howard:* No. Thank you.
>
>> *Customer Representative:* Please don't hesitate to call if anything else ever comes up. It is our pleasure to help you. Have a great day.

Obviously, I would have a very high opinion of the store and the way they handled my problem. I would also be very happy to let my friends and family know about the positive experience.

You want your clients to be your best source of advertising. You want them to tell their friends and family they have someone they trust, are happy with, and—most important—believe. When your client leaves your office, you want them to be relieved and stress free. You want your clients empowered.

You do all of that by keeping it simple.

Chapter Summary:
Keep Your Language and Processes Simple

- ✓ Not keeping it simple frustrates clients.

- ✓ Limit your use of jargon and be prepared to clearly and concisely explain terminology.

- ✓ Use the storyselling technique—telling a simple story that makes it easy for clients to relate to and understand.

- ✓ Keep your processes simple—it lowers client frustrations, enhances the client experience and increases your value to your client.

- ✓ Set your clients up for success. Make working with you a positive experience. Reduce stress points as much as you can.

> *"If people like you, they'll listen to you, but if they trust you, they'll do business with you."*
>
> —Zig Ziglar

CHAPTER 2

*Common Mistake:
Building a Client Relationship
on Selling a Commodity*

**Simple Idea:
Build a Client Relationship on Trust**

I BELIEVE THE MOST EFFECTIVE advertising of our services is word-of-mouth. Happy clients tell their friends and family about you, and they, in turn, want to tap into that financial happiness and peace of mind for themselves. They become willing to meet with the financial advisor. That is why I say happy clients are our best advocates.

How do we get happy clients? By realizing that our business relationships are not built on selling a commodity, they are built on trust. In fact, in my opinion 90 percent of a successful relationship is built on trust. Without trust, what kind of relationship do we really have with our clients?

Too often, clients describe their business relationship with their advisors as "fine." What they are really saying is that their expectations are so low that they are willing to accept the bare minimum. You don't want your clients to just feel "fine" about their working relationship with you. As we will cover throughout this book, you want clients who are strong advocates who will happily refer their friends, family and neighbors to you. You develop advocates through trust, and you develop trust through a strong, positive working relationship. That is why I have developed a process that sets right from the start what the client can expect when working with me.

Let's take a look at my process for building a working relationship on trust with a word-of-mouth referral client.

Initial Telephone Interview

Everything begins with an initial telephone interview. After getting the go-ahead from my existing client that their friend or family member is interested in speaking with me, I place a brief introductory phone call. Generally, the conversation lasts about five minutes. The purpose is to help me understand their situation and what their needs are.

I conclude this initial conversation with an overview of how I work with my clients. This includes bringing up the topic of compensation. Why do I bring up this potentially awkward topic so early in the process? Clients get nervous about how much a financial advisor's services will cost. By discussing compensation up front you eliminate a "hidden objection" for clients to change their mind about meeting with you face-to-face. Some advisors have cancellation rates of 20 to 50 percent because they don't mention compensation up front. The majority of cancelling clients say they can't make the appointment and will reschedule—but they never do. Because advisors think they will call they don't view it as a cancellation, so the cancellation rate might actually be significantly higher. Even if the appointment holds, the client is often wondering about fees throughout the meeting. We will go over many more specifics of compensation later on in this chapter, as well as in Chapter 6.

Once the potential client and I decide there is a mutual interest, then and only then do we move forward and schedule a face-to-face appointment.

Initial Face-to-Face Interview

I call this meeting an interview rather than the more common industry term *presentation* because I want my potential client to be engaged in the conversation, not left with the feeling of having been lectured. The purpose of the face-to-face interview is to learn about their family, their immediate needs and their long-range financial goals. If a couple, I try to arrange it so that I can meet with both parties at the same time to offset potential obstacles from initially meeting with only one partner.

I typically ask between one hundred and one hundred-fifty questions. The most important are the follow-up questions in response to their answers. Why? Because it is essential to put clients at ease and let them know that they are being heard. Among the questions I ask are:

- ☐ Are there any concerns of job security, or any consideration for changing jobs in the near future?

- ☐ How many children do you have? Is college for your children important to you? Have you already set up college funds?

- ☐ How much money have you saved and in what savings instruments?

- ☐ What kinds of investments do you have?

- ☐ What about retirement savings?

- ☐ How much debt are you carrying? Is it in the form of mortgages? Car loans? Credit cards? Student loans?

- ☐ Are you expecting a tax refund?

☐ How much insurance do you carry? Life? Homeowners? Long-term care?

Once I have an overall picture of the client's financial health, I ask questions about goals and dreams.

☐ When would you like to retire?

☐ How much money would you realistically like to have at retirement?

☐ What kind of retirement would you like to have? No work at all? Active and traveling? A soft retirement—meaning you will be working part-time?

Finally, I ask two more questions. The first is, "What kind of relationship are you looking for with the financial advisor you choose to work with?" The second question is, "Let's say it's five years from now and we are working together and I've done a great job for you. You are totally satisfied. Tell me, what exactly have I done for you?" The answers often help clarify the kind of relationship they want with me, as well as provide context to their other answers.

This series of questions establishes what is important to the client. Sometimes these are questions they have put off asking themselves out of financial insecurity. Sometimes each spouse might have a different idea of what they want in retirement, generating a conversation between them before arriving at a consensus.

Every once in a while I will get pushback from prospective clients asking why I need to know these very personal answers. I tell them that when it comes to their finances and their future, everything is interconnected. Another reason I ask these types of personal questions is that in answering them the client is building a bond of trust.

I conclude the interview by further explaining how I am compensated. *I want to stress that not talking about compensation in the first interview is the biggest mistake in successfully building a client relationship.* Potential clients often believe that having a professional financial advisor is more expensive or fee laden than they can afford or are willing to pay. For many potential clients, speaking with a financial advisor is almost as anxiety laden as buying a new car. People cover up like a boxer against the ropes, waiting to be taken advantage of. It is important to allay their fears and demonstrate in the long run that a professional advisor is a good investment. I also let them know that part of my compensation is not monetary, but comes in the form of future introductions and referrals. If I make them money, save them money, meet or exceed their expectations, then I would like them to be comfortable introducing me to family and friends—just as their friend or family member introduced them to me.

One point about referrals I'd like to make here is that sometimes you will get pushback. A client might say, "I don't give referrals." What they are really saying is, "I don't want to get blamed if my friend loses money." I respond by asking if they ever tell friends about a movie they love or a restaurant where they had a great meal. Most people, of course, say yes. I suggest that they think of telling others about me as more of an opinion based on their experience than as a referral. This approach helps make them more comfortable with the idea.

Finally, I stress that no decisions need to be made in this first interview. Instead, I let them know that I will take their responses and create a financial needs analysis. This document provides written recommendations of options and strategies, along with action steps to accomplish what they have told me is important to them.

To me, it's important that clients come away from the first interview believing that working with me creates value. Prior to the end of the first interview, I will introduce several money-saving or moneymaking ideas in concept, letting clients know that personalized details will come on the second visit. I want to get them thinking that working with me—or any professional financial advisor—gives them access to experience and information they would not normally get investing by themselves or listening to the advice of friends and family.

Here are some of the ideas that I present to them in the first interview:

> **Debt stacking**—Most people, once they pay off a debt, take the amount of that monthly payment they are no longer making and put it back into their budget as additional disposable income. Debt stacking puts that money to work for them and accelerates their paying down all of their debt. Here's how it works. Once you have paid off one debt, you take the amount of the monthly payment you had been making on it and add it to your monthly payment of your next debt. When the second debt is paid off, you add that to the third, and so on. This concept is sometimes also known as debt snowballing.
>
> **Retirement funds**—I'll discuss the different tax benefits of putting money in a Roth IRA or traditional IRA, or of increasing contributions. I'll also remind them to see if their employer offers a 401(k) matching payment.

Creating a Client Experience

After the initial face-to-face interview—and after every subsequent meeting and interaction—I want my clients to feel that they are getting an experience. It is part of your job, as a financial advisor, to make clients feel comfortable in entrusting their investments with you.

How do you make them feel comfortable? Remember that you are a customer every time you walk into a store or meet with a service provider. How do you like to be treated? What are the special, unexpected touches that bring you back again and again? Think about the answers to these questions and see how you can provide similar touches to your clients.

Storyselling:
Creating an Experience Creates a Loyal Customer

Let me share a story about the difference a positive experience can make. Several years ago, I was speaking with two friends. One of them said it was time for them to get a new car and this time they wanted a premium luxury car. The other friend said, "You should look at Lexus." "No," the prospective car buyer said, "I have my mind set on some other brands." "Trust me," the second friend said, "just check out Lexus." The friend agreed.

One week later we met for lunch. My friend was driving a brand-new Lexus. He told me that when he walked into the dealership he was greeted by the salesperson and welcomed to the "Lexus Experience." He was impressed that they had a whole process designed to show the strengths, the benefits and all of the wonderful things Lexus does that set the brand apart from the competition. He felt they really appreciated their customers in general and personalized the process in such a way that he felt appreciated individually.

As financial advisors, we can develop our own experience processes. The "Howard Lashner Experience" is based on giving my clients peace of mind. I explain to them right from the start what working with me is going to be like. They don't have to make any decisions on the first visit; this is very reassuring. Remember, clients are seeking someone they can trust with most, if not all, of their life savings—they don't want to feel pressured into making decisions before they are ready. Learning up front the form my compensation takes also eases their anxiety. Finally, they will have an opportunity to see things in writing and then decide from there.

Keep in mind that multimillion-dollar investors expect high-quality, personalized service. Investors at the million-dollar and under level too often receive "cookie cutter" experiences—and consequently, that is what they expect. By giving them an unexpected, highly personalized experience, you make them feel that they are very important clients. And you know what? They are.

More about Compensation

One reason many financial advisors don't discuss compensation early on in their process is they think they can wow prospective clients with their knowledge. Once clients are suitably impressed, advisors will discuss the fees, expecting the reaction to be, "Wow, you are worth it." It doesn't really work that way. In fact, in my experience, when I bring up my compensation early on, most clients breathe a sigh of relief. They are also more relaxed and able to pay close attention to what I advise and suggest.

I've stressed the importance of bringing up compensation early in the process, but how are financial advisors compensated, and which one is right for your client and you? There are four basic models.

1. **Pay for a Plan**

   The advisor, for a set fee, executes a financial plan of how money should be allocated. Often, clients can create a similar plan for free on many financial-service companies' websites. So why would clients pay for this service? Because a one-size plan doesn't fit all. Online, clients are asked preset questions and can't adjust the program for personalized assumptions. Financial advisors, however, can adjust the software to factor in new assumptions. This enables advisors to show clients how they can take actions toward their goals rather than feeling they are merely looking at a bunch of numbers.

2. Pay an Hourly Fee

Advisors charge an hourly fee for their services. The problem with this model is that clients become reluctant to call the advisor with questions or meet regularly because it will cost money. A good financial advisor will explain that asking important questions and meeting regularly will likely save clients money in the long run.

3. Pay a Commission

Advisors get paid an upfront commission, which is called an A share, from the investment company.

4. Pay a Wrap Fee (Managed Accounts)

Managed accounts are becoming the most common compensation model. In lieu of charging a transaction charge, the financial advisor will charge 1 to 2 percent of the investment assets per year.

BUILD TRUST AS QUICKLY AS POSSIBLE

The simple idea to overcome the common mistake of building a client relationship based on selling a commodity is to look for opportunities to build trust as early in the client relationship as possible.

A great way to think about how you can build trust is to consider situations where you, as a customer, felt trust in a service provider. Here is an example from my own life.

Recently my wife and I decided to put on an addition to our home. We asked our neighbors, friends and family for architect referrals and were given several names. We met with each one, but one architect stood out head and shoulders above the rest. Why? Liz figuratively held our hand throughout the process.

She walked the land with us where we planned to build the addition, checking the slope. She said we have to verify that our township doesn't have any ordinances against changing the slope or that the addition doesn't encroach too close to our neighbor's yard. We had provided each architect with a land survey we had previously done. Liz spent time going over it and felt that it lacked enough detail. So far, what Liz did tracked with what some of the other architects had done.

Now, here came her difference—and she presented it in a way that really built trust. She asked us to contact the original surveyors and started to give me questions to ask them. She was speaking in architectural jargon—words that were second nature to her but a foreign language to my wife and me. Our eyes must have glazed over with confusion, because Liz stopped herself and began to laugh. She suggested a three-way call among herself, the surveyor and me. I would give the surveyor permission to speak to Liz and she would ask the right questions to get the exact answers she needed to deliver the best possible service to her client: me. Liz said that she did not want me to spend money beginning the design-and-build process only to discover it can't be done.

I smiled in recognition. This is how I treat my clients. When necessary, we will do three-way calls to ensure that the right questions are asked to get the right answers that best benefit my clients.

My wife and I trusted that Liz was the best person to make our dream addition a reality. We were confident that she would protect me from the natural mistakes I could make entering into a world I didn't fully understand. She built our trust in her before we even saw architectural drawings—which, by the way, were wonderful.

Liz hit all of the markers of what I consider great client service—both as a client and as a provider.

- Great service means taking on responsibility rather than passing the buck to the client.

- Make things as easy as possible for clients—don't give them opportunities to think that you are disposable.

- Be responsive—many times clients will leave a message and say it's not that important to call back immediately. Call back as soon as you can—if it's important enough for them to call you, then it should be important to you to respond.

- Clients want to feel that someone is working in their best interest.

The process of a potential client becoming a client should occur before you even make a financial recommendation. When you build trust, clients know what to expect from you, and they feel certain that it is better than what they imagined or what they currently receive. Let me caution you, however, against mistaking the beginning of success for the end. I have seen too many financial advisors stop trying to build the relationship after the initial implementation of their program. This can be costly, because the true value of a client lies in the long-term, trusted relationship.

One of the most common complaints I hear when I meet with a new client is how they felt abandoned by their previous advisor. Here is a typical comment:

> *Client:* Our previous advisor was great—when we first met with her. She really sold us on how hands-on she would be. But after we moved our money into her recommended accounts, we rarely, if ever, heard from her. The accounts are doing fine, yet, when we need something, she tells us to call the toll-free number or go to a website because it will be quicker and easier if we take care of it ourselves. It's definitely quicker and easier for her!

Let's look at the mistakes this financial advisor made with her client.

- Over-promised and under-delivered a hands-on experience to her client.

- Failed to use follow-up communication.

- Didn't regularly consult with the client to capitalize on the success when the client's accounts were earning money.

- Emphasized technology and automation rather than personalized service.

These are all common mistakes, and we will look at many of these—and more—in the upcoming chapters. More important, I'll share with you actions I take to avoid or remedy these mistakes.

CHAPTER SUMMARY:
BUILD YOUR CLIENT RELATIONSHIP ON TRUST

- ✓ You want clients who are strong advocates; you develop advocates through trust.

- ✓ Start the relationship with an initial telephone interview.

- ✓ Bring up the topic of compensation early in the process; not talking about compensation in the first interview is the biggest mistake in building trusted relationships.

- ✓ Set up an initial face-to-face interview—think of it as an interview rather than a presentation; engage the client in the conversation.

- ✓ Ask questions about their immediate needs and long-term financial goals.

- ✓ Present money-saving and moneymaking ideas in the first interview.

- ✓ Deliver an experience to your client: The "Howard Lashner Experience" is based on giving my clients peace of mind.

- ✓ Build trust as quickly as possible by demonstrating to clients how you are working in their best interest.

- ✓ The true value of a client lies in the long-term, trusted relationship.

> *People don't buy WHAT you do, they buy WHY you do it.*
> —Simon Sinek

CHAPTER 3

Common Mistake:
Trying to Sell or Implement Your
Plan Right from the Start

Simple Idea:
Learn Client Concerns and What They
Want and Need—Then Deliver!

As we saw in Chapter 2, an important way to build trust is to eliminate pressure on clients at the first meeting. You want new or potential clients to feel comfortable and relaxed about meeting with you and discussing their finances. Some are going to come in feeling comfortable. Perhaps they have been handling their own finances for years, but some situations have changed and they want to speak with a professional. Some are terrified about their financial future and unsure about what they should do in the present. They know they need a financial advisor—they're just afraid of the whole process. And in some cases, one spouse knows more about their financial condition than the other, and they really don't want the other to learn the details.

Here is that type of situation, which I have encountered. When I started to ask questions of one couple about their debt, I noticed that the wife became visibly shaken. She took a deep breath and said, "Okay, he doesn't know this, but . . ." She then confessed to the credit-card debt she had run up. The important thing is that I do not make judgments. I don't react and say that's terrible or ask the husband how he feels about that. I acknowledge that it must have been difficult to tell me—and her husband—but it was important that she did. The first step to improving a situation is to know and accept exactly where we are.

Often, you can also ease their mind by assuring them that where they are, financially, is not as bad as where they fear they are. Recently, I met with a couple in their early sixties. They had become afraid that they would never be able to afford to retire and had visions of working as eighty-year-old store greeters or fry cooks. I calmly went through their finances, reassuring them that maybe they won't be able to sail off into the sunset on a yacht, but they will indeed be able to retire and live comfortably. I said that their goals were realistic and could be reached through some minor adjustments. There would be no heavy lifting needed. I gave them simple steps to follow, and by the end of the meeting they were relieved.

See the World Through Your Client's Eyes

Do you discuss financial solutions and choices with clients in a way that leaves them feeling they are making the choice based on your advice rather than feeling they are being "told" what to do?

When new or potential clients sit with a financial advisor, their concern is that the advisor is going to be pushing some products or their own agenda. I set their mind at ease through storyselling—letting them know that I've had similar fears as a client and that I understand. My architect story is a great example of that. The architect's job is to design my dream home, not hers. I let clients know that when I sit with them, my goal is to see the world through their eyes. What is the best choice I would make with their financial resources and my knowledge?

I also help them understand that what I am actually doing for them is taking ideas and concepts that are in the back of their mind and showing them how to apply them. I want them to see me as a guide to helping them reach the summit of their financial potential and to help steer them away from making emotional decisions.

I want them to truly feel that I have empowered them to be in control of their finances. At the same time I want them to feel that I am with them every step of the way, that it is "us against the world." That's why I use the term *our money* instead of *your money*.

Remember, you cannot and should not try to be all things to all people. As the old saying goes, "If all you have is a hammer, then everything will look like a nail." Know who your target market is and where you can create the most value. No one product or program is right for everybody. When you know that you are in front of the right client with the right program, then it is easy to convey your value.

HAVE A PROCESS TO LEARN CLIENT CONCERNS AND WHAT THEY WANT AND NEED

When driving to a client meeting I practice what I want to say to ensure I explain concepts as simply and understandably as possible. I also practice what questions I want to ask—not just the initial questions, but also the possible follow-ups.

Probably all financial advisors have an outline of what they are going to ask when they sit down with a client. The outlines are usually conceptually similar—questions about investments and debt. Of course, these are important questions to have clients answer, but *I maintain that the most important questions are the follow-ups you ask after the client responds*. Here is what I mean.

A simple question is, How much money do you have in your checking account? The client responds, "$100,000." You can enter that into the financial needs analysis document and you have an idea of their liquidity. But look how much more information you can get if you ask follow-up questions.

If you ask, How come you have that much money in your checking account? they might say, "I put an extra $1,000 into my checking account each month and it just keeps building and building." Okay, now I know that they have a lot of extra money per month in their budget that they can use to increase their 401(k) or IRA contributions or make additional investments. They could also use that money to pay down debt faster.

Perhaps their answer to how come they keep that much in their checking account is that they recently received a windfall through an inheritance or settlement and have parked it in checking until they can make a decision on what to do with it. You might ask the client questions like, Is that all the money or is there additional money coming in? If from an inheritance, was there something in the will about how to use it? Is any of this going to your children or into a college fund?

Maybe it's a work bonus. Are they expecting additional bonuses in the future? It could be that they get stock options every year and they sell them as they come due and there is a big payout. That's important to know, because this could be additional money on an ongoing basis.

Asking the right questions can also help attract future referrals. If the money is from an inheritance, are there siblings who also inherited the same or similar amount? If it's stock options at work or a generous bonus payout, then you could ask for introductions to coworkers who are in similar situations.

So, the key is really the question beyond the question.

Here is another example. If the person has a lot of credit-card debt, you ask, What caused this? If they say this has accumulated over the years, then we can talk about budgeting or changing their spending habits, or they might have an income issue where they just don't make enough to pay their bills. If they say the debt was run up quickly because there was a health issue and they paid medical expenses on credit cards, or they helped out a family member with some bills, then that tells you the debt was situational and not systemic. It is the question after the question that gives you a full picture of client financial health.

See the world through the client's eyes so they do not feel they are just looking at numbers on a piece of paper.

SHOW CLIENTS THE VALUE OF WORKING WITH YOU

Have you ever heard of "learned helplessness?" It is a psychology theory that describes a state of mind where people, based on their past experiences, feel helpless to avoid negative situations. It's a "damned if I do, damned if I don't" mentality. No matter what decision a person makes, they fear it is the wrong one. What does this have to do with someone's financial condition? More than you might realize.

Take for example someone who is overwhelmed by debt. They have a first and second mortgage, car loans, credit cards, personal loans and student loans. They might have a good income, but most of their money goes to debt service, leaving them in cash-flow binds, so they rack up more debt. They give up the hope that they'll ever be able to dig out of the hole, so they continue digging the hole. They will make bad financial decisions because they no longer feel that anything matters. They take the attitude that if they were going to be depressed about their finances, they'd rather be depressed while driving a new Mercedes-Benz than a fifteen-year-old Honda.

I will sometimes get "learned helplessness" clients because their friends or family members suggest they speak with me to help them break out of their predicament. My goal with this type of client is to help them start to unwind and decompress. I will say, I know that you felt overwhelmed—*I always put it in the past tense to plant the seed that things are now about to change*—but I am going to show you some very simple steps you can take to see the light at the end of the tunnel. Seeing the light at the end of the tunnel gives them hope. Your value as a financial advisor is getting them to see that light. You want all of your clients to feel confident and optimistic about their financial future and not feel that they have to make important decisions alone.

Of course, most clients don't suffer from a "learned helplessness" mentality. Many are already taking positive steps—some large, some small—toward financial health and comfortable retirement, yet still lack optimism about their financial future.

Storyselling:
Bob and Chris Plan Their Retirement

Bob and Chris have a goal to retire at age sixty-five with $6,000 per month of income. I go through their financial needs analysis and determine that to meet their goal they need to increase their savings from their current $600 per month to $2,000 per month. I know that if I hit them directly with that news they are going to lose hope that they'll be able to retire comfortably.

Instead, I focus on the actions they can take to make financial adjustments that bring them toward their goal. Here are some of the ideas I would present to them:

> **Retire at sixty-six, not sixty-five.** One year later can make a big difference. You get higher Social Security income; there's one less year of spending your retirement money; one more year of growth on your assets; and one additional year of saving.
>
> Instead of an income of $6,000 per month, reduce the goal slightly, to $5,700 or $5,800.
>
> **Consider a soft retirement.** Instead of working a forty-hour week, you can work a fifteen- to twenty-hour week. For some, part-time work and Social Security income means they don't have to touch their savings. A soft retirement of three years gives them three additional years of letting their savings and

investments grow. Conversely, it might work better for clients to work part-time and make withdrawals from their savings so they don't have to touch their Social Security until they are seventy, maximizing their amount. Every year that you delay Social Security, your payment goes up 8 percent.* By delaying it four years, you are looking at an almost one-third higher payment. That is a significant monthly boost.

As you can see, there are many options financial advisors can offer their clients based on their specific needs and goals. Our goal is to help them feel good about the process and feel empowered.

As I mentioned in Chapter 2, at the end of the first interview, I present clients with moneymaking and money-saving ideas that also demonstrate the value of working with a professional financial advisor. They leave the interview feeling relieved and comfortable and more hopeful about their debt or their retirement or whatever their specific concerns we have discussed. In our second meeting, I present them with specific details on how to implement these ideas to enhance their financial health.

Let's take a look at two examples of ideas I might present to clients that demonstrate the value of working with a financial advisor.

Storyselling:
Jorge and Luisa Debt Stack

Jorge and Luisa came to me with $100,000 in debt, not counting their first and second mortgages. They had twelve different credit cards and personal loans. They were in their mid-fifties and couldn't see their way out of debt and into a comfortable future retirement. In speaking with them, I learned they got a tax refund of approximately $7,000 per year.

---

* Source: www.ssa.gov Retirement Planner: Delayed Retirement Credits

Because they were in so much financial stress throughout the year, they would spend the refund on items they really didn't need as a reward for living "in deprivation" for most of the year.

    I ran the numbers for them and showed them that they could reduce debt by the time they were sixty-three—well ahead of their desired retirement age of sixty-six. Through the debt-stacking concept, Jorge and Luisa were able to reduce their debt. More important, they also changed their spending habits so that they didn't continue adding new debts to those already existing.

**CHAPTER SUMMARY:
LEARN AND DELIVER ON CLIENT
CONCERNS, WANTS AND NEEDS**

- ✓ Ease your client's mind through the assurance that where they are is not as bad where they fear they are.

- ✓ See your client's financial world through their eyes.

- ✓ Ask the most important questions—the follow-ups—after the client responds.

- ✓ Show clients the value of working with you—no matter how hopeless they may feel about their debt or financial future, get them to see the light at the end of the tunnel.

The cleanliness of theory is no match for the mess of reality.
—Bob Safford

CHAPTER 4

Common Mistake:
Trying to Do It All by Yourself

Simple Idea:
Develop an Administrative Staff—
Even If It's One Person

A MAJOR MISTAKE I HAVE seen financial advisors make is in believing that they can be a true one-man shop. Wrong, wrong, wrong. No matter the size of your business, you cannot –and should not—do it all yourself. There are just too many moving pieces in today's world. Going it alone can lead to missed opportunities and big mistakes.

A well-trained and knowledgeable administrative staff—even if it is a part-time staff of one—enables you to prospect for new clients and work directly, providing financial advice to existing clients while delegating to your staff appropriate client contact for paperwork and other administrative duties.

What are the benefits of having an administrative staff? They help you improve your client experience and build your credibility with clients, and they can be your eyes and ears.

Let's take a look at each benefit.

Improve Your Client Experience

Too many financial advisors suggest to their clients that they can take certain actions on their own via company websites. Actions like filling out forms and applications can be done online, but they can also be confusing and frustrating to fill out without guidance. Clients can sometimes make costly mistakes by making uninformed financial decisions. The mistake financial advisors make when suggesting clients take actions online is that they minimize their value to their client. The actions we may think are simple—like filling out forms—are often the actions clients stumble over.

I had a client who came to me because the advisor they were planning to work with sent them a blank, multi-page application, which daunted them. They never got around to filling out the application. Had the advisor taken the time to fill in the items he knew—name, address, etc.—the client would have felt more comfortable. You can be sure that is exactly what I did for this new client. It's better to learn from someone else's mistake than it is to make the same mistake yourself.

Build Credibility

Having the right answer isn't enough. You have to have credibility with the client. Everything I do and have my staff do is based around building credibility so that clients say yes.

Storyselling is a great way to build credibility. Tell new and prospective clients how you have successfully helped clients in similar situations. When I do this, I make sure that I describe clients that came to me in worse shape than the client in front of me.

There are two types of credibility financial advisors can build:

Knowledge Credibility—Clients must trust that you have the knowledge and know-how to help them make intelligent and informed decisions with their money. This is more than having degrees, licenses and certifications. They need to know that you have worked in situations similar to theirs and you have the needed experience to move forward in a positive direction. Using the storytelling technique is a great way to build trust, especially when you tell them about how you helped clients who were in worse financial situation then they are in.

Your staff can help build your knowledge credibility through how they communicate with clients. Whenever possible I prefer sending letters over emails. People hold on to the letter as a reminder; people rarely print out emails, and more often delete them after reading them. Another important reason why I prefer sending letters is that I don't want an email relationship with my clients. We are in a highly regulated industry and I don't want clients to send personal and banking information via email.

Integrity Credibility—Clients must trust that you will place their best interest ahead of your compensation. This is a big topic right now in the financial industry. There is an ongoing debate over how those who provide advice and recommendations on retirement accounts should be regulated and the types of standards to which they should be held. In general, there are two basic ways to look at this issue: The recommendation needs to be suitable for the client; and, the recommendation should be in the client's best interest.

How the industry and the regulatory agencies such as FINRA (Financial Industry Regulatory Authority) and the SEC (Securities Exchange Commission) choose to implement or merge these two ways is best left to those far more knowledgeable than I am. I will say, however, that regulations aside, every client wants to believe that their advisor is working with their best interest at heart.

Having an administrative staff trained to be responsive to your client's needs in a timely manner further demonstrates your integrity credibility.

Howard Lashner

Be Your Eyes and Ears

In many cases, assistants have more direct contact with clients than do the financial advisors. They take care of the administrative tasks, like change of address, adding direct deposit and changing banking information. A good assistant will also ask why changes are being made. Perhaps the client has left their job or is planning to take early retirement. That is something I need to know. My assistant will tell me, and I will reach out to the client to discuss what they are planning to do and what their financial options are. Sometimes simply brainstorming with a client can make all the difference, but I wouldn't know the situation if my assistant didn't ask questions and bring the answers to my attention.

The Role of an Administrative Assistant

When I get a new client, one of the first things I do is have my assistant call and introduce herself. I am comfortable doing this because my assistant, Christina, has earned both my trust and the trust of our clients. She has become my right hand and I view her more as my partner than my employee.

Christina tells the client that she now works for them. This is an important distinction that I firmly stress to both my assistant and clients. Assistants have to feel a connection with clients and be responsive to each communication; clients have to feel that they have a team working for them and that they are not making decisions alone. This makes clients feel comfortable that they have made the right decision and are more favorable to providing referrals.

Christina builds this comfort by demonstrating to clients that she has their back. She is always looking at what's in the client's best interest. She takes the responsibility to ensure that each client interaction goes smoothly and accurately. If there is any challenge, she makes sure it is handled properly to completion.

How can you ensure that your assistant is as client-focused as Christina? The most important thing you can do for all of your employees is demonstrate that your attitude is about serving and keeping the client happy. That means you have to walk the walk and talk the talk. If you talk poorly about your clients it will come through in your staff's attitude. You must have them understand that you may pay their salary, but they work for the client. The more work that needs to be done for the client the greater job security your staff has. If problems and follow-up never occurred, your staff would not be needed.

The assistant should start developing a relationship with a new client immediately. Here is my approach. I fill out the paperwork with the client, whether it is done online or as a paper application. I then discuss the application with my administrative staff for any client follow-up that needs to be done. Next, my assistant calls the client to introduce herself and give them her contact information.

This call serves several purposes. First, it helps give me—as well as my organization—credibility. Again, it is the idea that there is a team working for the client, and that there is one person—the financial advisor—who spearheads the team. My assistant might say something along the lines of "You are going to love working with Howard. All of his clients do. He's really dedicated to them. Anything you need, call us and he, or we, will get back to you quickly."

Second, the call lets the client know the assistant's role. "Every ninety days—unless Howard has something specific he needs to discuss with you—you'll hear from me as a follow-up to see if you have any questions or concerns. If you do, we'll make sure Howard is able to address them for you."

The assistant also walks the client through transaction processes. For example, if the client has just opened an IRA with a third-party mutual fund, the assistant can offer to set up a three-way call to verify that all the information and paperwork are complete, or the assistant can offer to help set up an online account so the client can track their funds. Again, it is my entire team's responsibility to create opportunities that alleviate client concerns and make their lives easier.

Developing an Administrative Staff

Developing a good staff is critical in building a successful, growing practice. Here are the steps I have taken with my staff.

Set Client Telephone Protocols

Most interactions between your client and your assistant take place over the telephone. That's why it is essential that you establish telephone-interaction protocols. Here are the clear standards I set with my staff:

- Answer the phone promptly.

- Return calls as quickly as possible. Clients may call with a question and say, "No rush, call back whenever you can." Handle it immediately; if it was important enough for them to call, it is important for you to provide a prompt response.

- Always do what you say you are going to do.

- Always call at the time you say you are going to call.

- Always offer to make three-way calls among yourself, the client and any third party. This alleviates client concerns about whether they will understand all the information or ask the right questions.

- Always be courteous and never be rushed.

- Give clients regular updates on anything that is outstanding that you are responsible for and that they are waiting to have happen. Typically, this involves money being transferred in or out of an account, so this is an important protocol to follow.

- Build a personal relationship with the client, even if it is only by phone. Stress with your staff that they represent you and your company in every conversation.

- Be careful with jargon; speak in plain English to ensure the client understands.

- Provide me with regular updates on all client interactions.

Have Daily Client Call Reviews with Your Staff

As I pointed out earlier, I believe it's important to provide clients with a memorable experience. To ensure clients are treated in the best possible way, I conduct a daily review of client calls with my staff. I ask them the following questions:

- Who called?

- What was their topic or issue?

- Has it been resolved? Was it resolved to their satisfaction?

- How do they now feel about the issue?

- Is there any follow-up required? On whose part? Mine? Yours (the administrative staff)? The client's?

▸ Is the required client action recorded? When there is necessary follow-up to be done by the client, it is recorded in our Client Relationship Management System. A reminder pops up on a selected date to check with the client that the action has been taken or needs to be taken soon. Having this system in place reinforces that an important part of my job and my admin's job is to help clients avoid mistakes.

What to Look for in an Administrative Staff

Remember the classic television show *M*A*S*H*? Whenever Colonel Potter asked for something, he would turn around and Corporal "Radar" O'Reilly would already be standing there with what he needed. How? "Radar" had duplicated the colonel's thought process.

That's what a great assistant does—duplicate your thinking. It is what my assistant does for me. She knows which clients I will be seeing and what paperwork or information I will need, and she will ask if there is anything else I need before the meeting. She is always very specific. She knows the exact order in which I want the paperwork and every brochure that I want.

An administrative assistant's job is more than merely managing paperwork. It is also to make my life easier and be an extension of me to clients. Outside of office hours my staff is each their own person. But during working hours they represent me to the client, so they have to make me—and our entire organization—look good.

One of my favorite quotes is from author Napoleon Hill, who wrote, "There are two types of people who never get ahead in life; one is a person who can't do what they're told to do; the second is a person who only does what they're told to do."

When hiring, I seek people who do get ahead in life, and in my experience these people are great listeners and have great initiative. They also share the qualities of being organized and being quick mental processors.

What do I mean by quick mental processors? They closely listen to what the client is saying—as well as what the client might not be saying—and can immediately grasp what's wrong and suggest resolutions. A good assistant understands that part of the job is to protect the client—sometimes from the client's own thinking.

Here is an example of quick mental processing. A client, age fifty, calls and says she wants to withdraw $10,000 from her taxable IRA. The assistant knows that the client has two accounts, one IRA and one individual account. The assistant suggests that, before withdrawing any money, the client speak to the financial advisor about how taking funds from the individual account might save on taxes and penalties.

Another thing I seek in an assistant is a thick skin. I can't afford to have someone who takes things personally. I have to confess that sometimes dealing with me can be difficult because I have a lot of things to do, a lot of things on my mind, and I am very task oriented. That's another reason why having a reliable assistant can make your life easier. Here is a typical telephone conversation I might have with my assistant, Christina, following a client meeting:

Christina: Hi, Howard.

Howard: This is a brain dump. Grab a pen and paper.

Christina: Okay, I'm ready.

Howard: I just left a meeting with the Smiths and I have a big to-do list that we need to get done as follow-up. First, we're going to be opening a Roth IRA for each of them. They will be funded with a one-time check from each. Second, we need to increase their 529 plan contributions from $200 per month to $400 per month. I want to schedule a three-way call on that. Third, I want you to put into their notes that Mary is pregnant and expecting in June.

At the end of the year they are going to be moving and he's going to be changing jobs. Lastly, his father is in ill health and there will be an inheritance. That's a conversation we will need to have down the road.

You get the idea. I can go on like this for five minutes just expressing a torrent of ideas and to-do items. Christina will take notes, only interrupting if something needs clarification. Once completed, I'll take a deep breath and say, "Okay, how are you doing?" I need an assistant who does not take personally my business-first approach.

Clients also often take a business-first approach when calling. Money is a sensitive, stressful topic for many people. When clients call, it's often related to some mistake or misunderstanding in paperwork, or an unexpected and stressful financial situation—an IRS letter, a medical emergency, or a home renovation that can no longer be put off. In these situations, clients can be very tough and direct with your staff. "Why is there a delay on funds transferring to my account?" or "I'm meeting with my accountant in two days. Why haven't I received my 1099-DIV forms yet?" Great assistants serve as a calming force for stressed clients.

A great assistant is also very flexible in terms of hours. For whatever reason, it seems like clients call at the end of the day, especially on Fridays, when it's almost impossible to reach any third-party company with whom their issue might be. Nonetheless, whenever the client calls the assistant has to have the flexibility to stay until we have done everything we can for the day.

One last but not least attribute I like to see in assistants is the ambition to get their own life insurance and securities licenses. There are lots of things assistants can do and assist in without a license, but that extra 10 percent of having a license makes a huge difference.

DOWNSIDE OF NOT HAVING AN ADMINISTRATIVE STAFF

When you take on all responsibilities for yourself, it's only natural that it impacts the quality of your life. There are always phone calls to answer, letters and emails to return, calls to third-party companies on behalf of your clients and so on. In and of themselves, none of these responsibilities is overly difficult or time consuming, but taken in aggregate, they can dominate the bulk of your day, leaving little time for your personal life, and more important, little time for talking with new and potential clients.

That brings me to another important downside: Not having a staff often means earning less money. That might seem counterintuitive given that you are not paying an employee or employees. Why would you earn less money?

There are just so many hours in a day. When you have someone to assist you, you can stay in your wheelhouse and specialize. The wheelhouse for most financial advisors is in developing new clients and working with existing ones growing their portfolios. Why take on tasks that keep you from your specialization? A surgeon doesn't wheel in the patient. The patient and equipment are ready for her when she enters the operating room. The surgeon performs her specialty because her time is valuable. Her surgical team handles the other tasks. I suggest you think like a surgeon. Focus on your specialty and let your team handle the other tasks.

Not having an administrative staff also affects your credibility with clients. Clients get concerned: "What if I need something taken care of and you're on vacation, or sick or not around?" They may not express this directly, but if they call in the morning and say they want to take some money out of an account or change their monthly investment amount, and you are booked solid for the entire day and can't call them back or take care of the item until the next day, they wonder if you've forgotten about them. Having a staff means someone can get back to them quickly and take care of their needs, eliminating any anxiety.

One final downside to consider is that without an administrative staff you do not have anyone who can build relationships with their counterparts at third-party companies. A good assistant gets to know department supervisors and builds relationships behind the scenes. They find ways to get things done in ways that you, as a one-person shop, don't have time to discover.

The biggest objection to hiring a staff I hear from financial advisors is that they don't have enough clients to warrant the expense of hiring an assistant. That is mistaken thinking. I strongly believe the reason I have been able to build a large, successful practice is because of my amazing assistants. Think about this: Isn't your time worth the hourly rate you would pay an assistant?

Storyselling:
A Tale of Two Assistants

An assistant is only as good as their capability to treat the client with respect and deliver on the client's needs. Here is an experience that Jane, a client referral of mine, had that illustrates how a bad assistant can make a difficult situation worse.

Jane's husband died shortly after he retired. He had handled all of their finances and it was an absolute mess trying to figure out everything. Her husband's advisor had always talked down to Jane and she felt she couldn't trust him. One of my clients suggested Jane talk to me.

Here is what she told me about her husband's advisor. First, she could not reach him by telephone. He was never in and didn't return her calls. Finally, his assistant called Jane. She turned out to be of little help.

The assistant, whose tone and attitude was very abrupt, said Jane's husband had nine different accounts scattered among several mutual-fund companies. She then gave Jane the toll-free numbers for each company and told her to call. The assistant then emailed Jane the paperwork needed to access and transfer the funds; each page was blank. Jane was overwhelmed. She called the assistant once again asking for help; but this time Jane was given the wrong tax information and dollar amounts. Even when she called the toll-free numbers, some of the representatives gave her inaccurate information. All of this misinformation delayed settling the estate. What was a very difficult time for this widow was made even worse because of a lack of caring on the part of the administrative assistant.

Here is how a capable, well-trained assistant would handle the situation.

> ***Assistant:*** I am so sorry for your loss. Your husband was a good client of ours. We will do everything we can to make this time easier for you.
>
> > ***Jane:*** Thank you so much. I need to transfer the accounts into my name.
>
> ***Assistant:*** Of course. You have two options: I can mail you the paperwork, or you can come into the office. What is easier for you?
>
> > ***Jane:*** I'd like to take care of it at your office.
>
> ***Assistant:*** Fine. I will prefill the information we already know—address, account numbers and the like. The rest we can fill in together. And then I'll mail in the forms for you.
>
> > ***Jane:*** Thank you. I really appreciate your help.

I estimate the assistant would have spent perhaps sixty minutes taking care of this for the client, who, for her part, would have spent thirty minutes maximum at the office. Jane would have been relieved—and would have had no reason to bring her business elsewhere.

There is no substitute for considerate, personalized service in keeping clients happy. In the next chapter I will cover the importance of a high-touch, personal experience, but for now remember that having a well-trained assistant enhances the experience you deliver to your clients.

Good Assistants Are Worth Their Weight in Gold

For the first ten years of my business I did 100 percent of the administrative work. I knew every piece of paper and every moving part of client relationships. As I gained more clients, the administrative demands took up more and more of my time. I became overwhelmed. I found it impossible to stay up on everything and be able to do the most important part of my business—providing financial advice and recommendations to my clients.

Once I hired an assistant, I expanded my mind-set about the role she should play. I thought of her as a partner whose job is to make my life easier and make my business and me look good to clients. With the passing of time our working relationship has deepened, and she has been able to duplicate my thinking, which helps improve the client experience.

In addition to duplicating the financial advisor's thinking, a good assistant knows more about the day-to-day business—because they take care of the administrative duties every day. They understand the third-party websites, the shortcuts, and who to speak to directly to get the right answers at the right time.

Of course, that doesn't mean the financial advisor doesn't have to pay attention to these sorts of details. It is your business and you have to always be thinking about it—especially when you have a great assistant who takes care of so much. The way I see it is that you have to *inspect what you expect*.

What do I mean by that? You need to have a system of ongoing communication where you make sure things are getting done. You don't want to discover weeks or months or even years later that something has fallen through the cracks and you weren't aware because you assumed someone was taking care of it. One of my rules is that whenever I ask my staff to do something, they must report back to me that it was done.

Also, from time to time, I do office spot checks, opening envelopes, looking at different files and asking questions. This is not because I do not trust my assistants. On the contrary, it is because I trust that so much gets done. The spot checks provide an insight into how things are done. Every once in a while I come across a situation and say, "Let's do this differently," or "Whenever this topic comes up, bring it to my immediate attention."

My assistants have learned that I don't need to be involved in everything, but there are times when my knowledge and experience are necessary. As the financial advisor it is your responsibility to make sure that things are taken care of—and done in the right way—for your clients. You don't have to stand over your staff or watch them like a hawk—but you do have to verify that things are done.

Another advantage to having a good assistant is they can serve as a backup calendar to ensure meetings or follow-up actions are met. Here is something that comes up from time to time. I'll see an article or receive some information that I believe would benefit a client. I'll tell my assistant that I want to call the client and run the idea by him, but I first need to do some additional research. I'll ask her to remind me in two days to call. I make a mental note to call, knowing that I will be doing the research over those two days, while my assistant writes down the reminder and lets me know when it is time to reach out to the client.

When there are specific client tasks that need to be completed on a timely basis, my assistant will also follow up with a reminder to make sure I actually took care of the item.

Another thing I do, which I believe is extremely important to continuous development of the administrative staff, is I hold regularly scheduled staff meetings. The topics we generally discuss cover:

- What we think is going right.

- What can be done better.

- What help they may need from me.

- The areas that create the greatest stress for them.

- How we can provide even better service to our clients.

Finally—and I believe this is something that must be stressed—when developing an assistant you must model the behavior you want them to have. If you complain about clients, the questions they ask, the workload you have to take care of, and that client calls interfere with getting things done, then that is the behavior the assistants will model when you are not around.

If you have an assistant with a bad attitude, before you confront them take a moment to reflect on your own behavior. Are they modeling you? If they have been, then talk to them about how you have been sending the wrong messages to them regarding clients and that you will both have to change your attitudes. If they have not been modeling you, then let them know in no uncertain terms that clients are not an impediment to business getting done; clients are the business. Speaking with clients, delivering on their needs and helping them feel happy is what we do. I've said this before and I cannot say it enough, if something is important to clients, it is important to us. That is the attitude everyone in your business must take.

CHAPTER SUMMARY:
DEVELOP AN ADMINISTRATIVE STAFF

- ✓ Trying to do everything yourself can lead to missed opportunities and big mistakes.

- ✓ Administrative assistants help improve your client experience, build your credibility with clients and act as your eyes and ears with clients.

- ✓ Assistants must understand that you may pay their salary, but they work for the client.

- ✓ When developing an administrative staff, it's important to set client telephone protocols and have daily client call reviews

- ✓ A great assistant duplicates your thinking.

- ✓ A great assistant should be a quick mental processor.

- ✓ Not having a staff often means earning less money; when you have an assistant, you have the time to specialize in what you do best.

- ✓ Good assistants are worth their weight in gold.

> *People do not buy goods and services. They buy relations, stories and magic.*
> —Seth Godin

CHAPTER 5

Common Mistake:
Relying Too Heavily on High Tech
Instead of High Touch

Simple Idea:
More Personalization, Less Automation

"Your call is very important to us and will be answered in the order it was received. A representative will be with you shortly Please do not hang up." We've all heard these words followed by the most horrible music, which only seems to be playing to make you want to hang up the phone in frustration. Then, when you are at last out of the queue, you are confronted with an automated voice asking you to select from the following options—none of which sound like the reason you are calling.

While there is a place for using toll-free numbers for easily taken care of items, too much reliance on your clients to do things via toll-free numbers and websites is the exact opposite of personalized service. Nonetheless, there is a move in the finance industry—as in many other industries—to minimize personal contact as much as possible in the transaction. The idea behind shifting clients to using websites and toll-free numbers is to make transactions cheaper, faster and empowering for the client to get the information when they want it.

What technology and automation doesn't do is build a trusted, long-term relationship. Here is a story you to which you might relate.

> ### *Storyselling:*
> ### Company Mistake—Client Headache

Not too long ago I noticed an error on my mobile-phone bill. I called the company and immediately reached the automated voice system. I punched 0 to bypass and go to a live operator, but 0 was not an option. Instead I was routed back to the beginning and had to listen to eight options that did not pertain to me before hearing that I could press 9 to speak with a representative. After several minutes of listening to cheery music that did little to cheer me up, I finally reached a representative. I explained the billing error and he told me that he would have to research the situation and get back to me. I asked for his name and a direct contact number. He could only provide his first name and there was no direct number, only the toll-free number. He promised someone would get back to me.

No one did. Two weeks later I started the process all over again and was told there was no record of the first call. I asked to speak to a supervisor, but there was none available. The representative promised a supervisor would call me back. I was so frustrated that I told the representative that I wanted to cancel my contract and take my business elsewhere. Unfortunately, the cancellation fee was still in effect.

Later that day, the supervisor called back and resolved the error, which could easily have been resolved during my initial call. I have not yet changed providers, but when someone asks who my provider is and would I recommend them, I can only say, if customer service is important to you, then I can't recommend them.

This story also points out an additional important thing technology and automation generally does not do—create raving fans: the happy, engaged clients who refer their friends and family to you. "Raving Fans" is an idea presented in the book of the same title by Ken Blanchard, a renowned business consultant and writer. Blanchard and his co-author, Sheldon Bowles, maintain that stunning customer service is a competitive advantage. This is as true for Fortune 500 companies as it is for your business.

In previous chapters I gave examples of clients who came to me after receiving poor client treatment from other advisors. I have also stressed the importance of referrals, which I strongly believe should be viewed as part of our compensation. Developing clients who love working with you for reasons above and beyond the investment gains you may have helped them get is how you retain clients and bring in new business. These clients are fully engaged and generate the word-of-mouth advertising that is essential to sustaining and growing your business. With the prevalence of social media, a positive tweet, Facebook post or Yelp review reverberates far and wide. Unfortunately, so do negative comments.

If you want to deliver an experience to your clients, as we looked at in Chapter 2, then you have to amplify the human touch and know when it is the right time to use technology and automated solutions. After all, when people are investing their life savings, they naturally have a lot of insecurity. They want a human hand to hold. As we saw in Chapter 4, having a talented, well-trained administrative staff goes a long way to delivering a personalized experience and creating engaged clients.

THE BENEFITS OF HAVING ENGAGED CLIENTS

Increased business: Not only are engaged clients more likely to provide referrals, they are also more likely to increase the amount and type of business they do with you.

Greater compensation: More business with individual clients means more income. More referrals also mean greater compensation.

More and better referrals: Happy, engaged clients are more likely to refer friends, neighbors and family members with higher net worth.

More trust in you: The more they trust your advice, and working with your administrative staff, the likelier it is that you will have a lifelong client.

An easier relationship: Having happy, engaged clients doesn't mean problems and issues don't arise, but when they do, the client's attitude is often more positive that you will take care of it in a timely and correct fashion.

Self-esteem: Everyone wants to feel good about the job they do. Financial advisors are no different. Knowing that you have developed happy, engaged clients increases your self-esteem and provides the positive attitude that helps maintain and grow engaged clients.

Differentiate yourself from the competition: Raving Fans are the best source of word-of-mouth advertising. They can help provide you with the reputation in the market as the financial advisor with happy clients.

THE BENEFITS OF BEING AN ENGAGED CLIENT

A sense of comfort and ease: Happy, engaged clients—even during times of economic ups and downs—feel secure that their investments are in the right hands.

Confidence about the future: They see the various pieces of their financial future fall into place. They also see this not only via monthly or quarterly statements, but through the regular personal communication they receive from you and your administrative staff.

Desire to do more business with their financial advisor: They are more inclined to consolidate their investments with you instead of spreading them out among multiple advisors because they see that you do the "little things" that count toward a great client experience.

Great feeling about the relationship: While money is often a sensitive topic among friends and family, people do have a tendency to vent about bad experiences with financial advisors. Your engaged clients are happy to tell friends and family that they have had a great experience with their advisor.

Storyselling:
A Personalized Strategy an Algorithm Can't Provide

A while back I began working with Paul and Betty, a couple in their thirties. They were smart go-getters, who, when we started working together, earned about $100,000 a year combined. Over the next five years their combined annual income rose to more than $500,000. At that time, they excitedly told me that they were saving $50,000 a year and that they were happy with their investments.

Of course, I was glad for them, but as their financial advisor I had a suggestion: Increase savings by another $10,000 per month. Needless to say, their eyes widened, their jaws dropped and they asked, How could they save that much more? I reminded them that only five years earlier they were living comfortably and paying their bills on $100,000 income. "You're making five times that amount, and I see that your expenses have not increased by five times the amount," I told them. I pointed out that they had now reached a point in their lives where they could really build for their future. To do that, however, meant thinking about what they needed versus what they wanted. They agreed to give it a try and save $10,000 a month more.

They successfully did so for the next six years, putting together a considerable amount of cash reserves. Their investments also continued to do well. Around this time they called to say they wanted to meet with me face-to-face to discuss a financial opportunity that had come their way. I went to their home and they told me about an opportunity for a career change—they would be working together—that had the potential to be worth millions of dollars in the long term. However, it would mean an immediate and significant pay cut. They would not be able to continue putting aside additional money into savings.

By this time Paul and Betty had saved a considerable sum, and now being in their forties, were still young enough to have many years of income and savings opportunities ahead. I suggested that it would be okay for them to stop saving for the next two to three years while they take the pay cut that they believed would lead to long-term income gains.

They were both relieved and made nervous by my advice: relieved that they could afford to go for this opportunity; nervous because they enjoyed saving and watching their money grow. I reassured them that they had done such a strong job on the front end that they could cut back now.

They took the opportunity and the pay cut, and four years later they sold a piece of the business they helped start for millions of dollars. Had they not originally started to aggressively save and invest fifteen years earlier, they would not have been in the position to take this opportunity. Because they had saved enough money at their stage in life, they could take a risk they believed could yield high rewards.

The advice I was able to give them—from originally increasing their monthly savings by $10,000 to showing that they could afford to take a short-term pay cut in the hopes of long-term gains—came from the time I spent with them over the years, getting to know their goals, dreams and needs. Clients cannot get that kind of advice by going onto a website. An algorithm doesn't understand goals and dreams. Calling a toll-free number won't provide strategies or insights. Technology and automation cannot create Raving Fans.

> ## *Storyselling:*
> ## Provide Your Clients with Financial Health Checks

People have more access to financial information than at any other time in history. They can watch finance and business networks on cable television. They can access how markets around the world are doing in real time via the Internet. There are personal-finance magazines, websites and podcasts where people give opinions and tout financial products and instruments.

Knowledge is only as valuable as your knowledge of how to use it.

Often, I will get a call from a client who has seen something on television or read something online and thinks it might be a great investment. Occasionally, after doing some research, I will agree. More often than not, I will tell my client that it is too high risk for an investor like yourself, or for where you are at this life stage. I tell them that I know how they are emotionally wired—they are going to stress over the risky investment. Nearly every time they will agree—since they also know how they are emotionally wired. Having the sounding board of a trusted financial advisor creates reassurance and reduces stress.

The best way for me to know their emotional makeup is to do periodic financial health checks, sort of a mini financial needs analysis. Before making recommendations, I look at their present situation, including their needs and wants. Then I will ask them questions that a Robo Advisor is not programmed to ask:

> Why do you want to make this particular investment now?

> Are you in need of increased investment income?

> Are you prepared to take a significant loss (if this is a high-risk investment)?

Have you thought about these options?

Automation can reduce costs by eliminating human touch. For the company, you create generic assumptions that eliminate paying for advice and experience. For the client, they can just "set it and forget it" by doing the transaction online.

What technology and automation will never be able to do is create the inestimable value of personal relationships between client and advisor built over time and built on trust.

Chapter Summary:
More Personalization, Less Automation

- ✓ The idea behind shifting clients to using websites and toll-free numbers is to make transactions cheaper, faster and client empowering.

- ✓ Technology and automation do not create "Raving Fans."

- ✓ Delivering a client experience means amplifying the human touch and knowing when to use technology and automated solutions.

- ✓ Engaged clients yield increased business, greater compensation and more and better referrals.

- ✓ Engaged clients feel a sense of comfort and ease with their financial advisor; they desire to do more business with their advisor.

- ✓ Providing your clients with regular financial health checks.

- ✓ Technology and automation will never be able to develop a relationship between client and advisor built over time and on trust.

> *"Nothing influences people more than a recommendation from a trusted friend."*
> —Mark Zuckerberg

CHAPTER 6

*Common Mistake:
Not Properly Setting the Stage for
References and Introductions*

**Simple Idea:
Make Yourself Referable**

In Chapter 2 we spent time looking at why I place importance on referrals as part of client compensation. In this chapter, I want to show you how to go about requesting referrals and introductions from your clients.

The best way of course is to make yourself referable. Clients have to trust you when you are asking for a referral or introduction. Asking for referrals is a very personal thing. People feel their credibility is at stake. The last thing they want—and the last thing you want to have happen—is for their family member or friend to tell them what a terrible experience they had with the financial advisor they recommended.

So, what are the actions you can take to make yourself more referable and give people more confidence in recommending you?

Treat Time Like a Valued Luxury

How many times has a business associate or client said to you, "I'll call you at nine," and at 9:10 there still has been no call. Frustrating, right? You really can't do very much in those ten minutes. If you want to make a call, you're not comfortable doing so because you're expecting to receive a call at any minute. Take care of paperwork? Same thing. Those are ten unproductive minutes. For busy people like us—and like our clients—wasted time is a lost commodity; and these days time is a luxury that should not be squandered.

I make sure that I demonstrate to my clients that I value their time.

When I have an appointment at 9:00, I am there at 9:00. My clients often comment with a laugh at on how precise I am. Some also ask, How do I do that, especially if I am coming from a half-hour or hour's drive away? Here is how I work that out: If the appointment is at 9:00, I plan to get there by 8:45. I park down the road and use the time to make some calls or review my notes. At 8:55 I park at the client's home or office, and at 9:00 I am knocking on their door. Why am I so devoted to this level of precision? As I tell my clients, "If you can't trust me with your time, how can you trust me with your money?"

Do What You Say You'll Do

Many years ago I attended a large convention. There were thousands of people there to network and exchange information. Time was spent in conversation and in promised follow-ups. I would ask someone about an issue or a product and receive replies such as, "I'll email it to you when we get back," or "I'll have my assistant mail it to you," or "I'll give you a call next week." Those replies were the only things I received from about 95 percent of the people with whom I spoke. I realized how few people actually do what they say they are going to do. I made up my mind not to be one of those people. If I say I am going to do something, then I am going to do it.

But how was I going to do it? Like most financial advisors—and most people in general—I had been making the mistake of relying on my memory. If I told someone I would call them in an hour, I'd log it in my head to call that person in an hour. Then I'd get busy doing other work, or receive or make other calls, and an hour or two or three would pass before I remembered to make that call.

Instead of logging it in my head, I put it in my phone calendar with a timed reminder to make the call in one hour. If the to-do item is more detailed than one phone call, I will call or text my assistant to remind me to follow up on the item. How important is doing what you say you'll do in making yourself referable? I spend an entire chapter on the subject later on in this book.

BE REALISTIC WITH YOUR CLIENTS

We are all well aware that when it comes to mutual funds and other investment instruments, past performance is not a guarantee of future performance. Do not promise the world to your clients. Just because a mutual fund has been averaging 12 percent growth a year doesn't mean that you will double your money in six years. Be realistic with your clients. Let them know that what a high-performing mutual fund indicates is confidence in the management and philosophy of the fund. It does not indicate doubling your money. Believe me, I have been around long enough to know that eventually, Murphy's Law kicks in. Whatever can go wrong will go wrong. That's okay—as long as you assure your clients that you will work through things together if a crisis occurs.

When the market has significant downturns, as it did in 2001 and 2008, and people start to panic, they not only expect their financial advisor to be available, they also want the advisor to be a calming voice of reassurance. If that means having to handle important items while on vacation, I will do so. Once again I will repeat one of my most important best practices: If it is important to my clients, it is important to me.

PEOPLE WILL TALK

As I previously have written, word-of-mouth is the best form of advertising. Make sure you get glowing reviews. If someone is going to take the time to recommend you, the person to whom they make the recommendation is likely going to let them know of the experience—good or bad. How do you make sure your client receives positive feedback from the new referral? While many factors as to whether or not investments make money or your advice saves clients' money are beyond your control, there are specific actions and attitudes that you can take that are totally under your control. Here are actions and attitudes that I take that have proven effective in making me referable:

- Don't be pushy. Take your time in making recommendations; do your research and show your reasoning.

- Your referral client is a different person from the one who made the referral. What worked for your original client may not be right for the new client. Don't be aggressive in your recommendations if they are financially conservative, and vice versa.

- Don't overstep your bounds. Assess the types and levels of advice the new client is seeking.

Taking these actions—as well as valuing their time and doing what you say you will do—greatly increases your chances of creating happy clients who will likely thank your original client for the introduction. And your new clients are likely to refer their friends and family.

Have Patience in Receiving Client Referrals

When I first start working with clients, I averaged about four prequalified referrals and introductions in the first year—by prequalified I mean that the client has spoken to their friend or family member and they have agreed to have a telephone conversation with me. Some of these first-year referrals lead to new clients, some don't. That's okay; because what I have discovered is that *the very best referrals come from clients you have been working with for years.*

Here is an example. After five years of working together, my client Meredith called to tell me that her very successful brother had been looking for a new advisor. He had seen the financial security Meredith had been building over the past five years and was interested in meeting with me. Meredith had also been telling him for years that I was extremely consistent, always did what I said I was going to do, and delivered on making and saving her money. I met with her brother, and he is also now a client—and a Raving Fan!

The only way to get long-term, quality referrals is to nurture and build your existing client relationships and continue to make yourself referable. When you ask people to trust you with their life savings, you need to be flawless in your execution and respectful of your client's time and money.

CHAPTER SUMMARY:
HOW TO MAKE YOURSELF REFERABLE

- ✓ Treat time like a valued luxury.

- ✓ Do what you say you'll do.

- ✓ Be realistic with your clients.

- ✓ Give them something terrific to talk about—it's not just about the money you make or save them; it's about your integrity and the experience you provide.

- ✓ Be patient in expecting to receive client referrals—the best referrals often come years down the road.

> *What we have here is a failure to communicate.*
> —from the movie *Cool Hand Luke*

CHAPTER 7

Common Mistake:
Not Doing Regular Customer Follow-Up

Simple Idea:
Create a Systematic Client Follow-Up Relationship

When I begin working with new clients, I discuss the type of follow-up they expect from me and how often. I always suggest that I contact them every ninety days, which corresponds to the timing of quarterly investment reports; if that seems too often to them, then I suggest every six months at minimum. Around the agreed-upon time, my assistant or I will call and ask if the client has any questions or concerns that need to be addressed. Often, the client neither answers nor returns the call. It doesn't matter. Keep calling regularly. Leaving a message demonstrates that you are reaching out and are available to address questions, concerns or needs whenever they may arise. Regular, systematic communications send a much different and stronger message to the client than merely saying at the beginning of the relationship, "Call me anytime if you need anything." Here is a wonderful example of what just might happen if you make regular follow-up calls.

Storyselling:
Simple Idea—Follow Up Regularly NO MATTER WHAT

A very successful advisor I know told me this story from her experience. She opened a small $5,000 investment account for a new client. She would call the client every ninety days—as she did all of her clients—to ask if she had any questions, concerns or anything that had to be addressed. She did this regularly for twelve years. Here is the odd thing about those ninety-day calls to this client—it was NEVER a live conversation. The advisor would never reach the client and would leave a message; the client would never return the calls. Since the phone number was apparently still good and the financial statements were never returned to sender, the advisor continued to make the regular calls just in case the client might one day need something.

That day finally came. The client called the advisor to let her know that she had just inherited several hundred thousand dollars. She said she was getting a lot of recommendations from friends about who should handle her investments, but the client said she wouldn't think of changing her relationship with the advisor. She said the advisor was the only person she would trust with her money because of the respectful way she had been treated all those years.

The advisor did not make those regular calls in the hopes that this client would one day come into hundreds of thousands of dollars. She made the calls because regular follow-up is the best practice, no matter what.

Of course, this is not a typical example of what might arise from regular follow-up, but it clearly demonstrates the value in regularly following up with clients. Now let's take a look at an example from my own experience of the potential cost of not following up.

> ## *Storyselling:*
> ## My Mistake in Not Following Up

Early in my career I helped a client open up a $50-per-month IRA. They were a couple in their early thirties; I was still in my twenties. They had never before invested, so I walked them through the process. Once their IRA was set up, I said if you ever need additional investments, give me a call.

Over the years I would see their account in my files. Their IRA account was growing and doing well. They didn't call me and I didn't follow up with them. Finally, as I developed my business and my skills, I realized that I had not spoken to these clients in seven years. By this time, I was developing my philosophy of working closely with clients and following up regularly on a quarterly basis. It was way past time to reach out.

I spoke with the husband, who said he and his wife were happy with how their IRA with me was doing. He mentioned that he had changed jobs. This is the conversation that followed:

Howard: Didn't you have a retirement plan at your old company?

Client: Yes.

Howard: What did you do with it?

Client: I rolled it over to an IRA I set up with my bank.

Howard: Why did you go with the bank if you were happy with the performance of the investments I recommended?

Client: Oh, I didn't realize you handled big investments. I thought you just handled the $50-a-month types of investments you helped us with.

The amount he rolled over with the bank in 1991 was about $80,000. While he kept the original IRA with me because it continued to perform well enough, he never moved the money from the bank or opened up any other investments with me.

This taught me an important lesson. Stay active in your client's financial life. It isn't just how much money a person has today; it is the lifetime relationship that is of value. I cannot afford to be shortsighted and transactional in how I think about my business. The attitudes of "if you have money, I will help you invest, then I'm done and on to the next client" or "if you have additional money to invest, let me know" are not the attitudes of long-term success.

By learning from mistakes such as this one, I have been able to build a successful career and the philosophy that I am sharing with you in this book.

Effective client follow-up goes well beyond regular telephone calls or the timely return of client calls and emails. It requires being a great listener, having a deep understanding of your client's ever-changing needs and wants, and, above all, being proactive. This is where building client relationships on trust; learning client concerns, wants and needs; doing periodic financial health checks with clients, using your administrative staff to serve as your eyes and ears; and creating a personalized client experience can help you maximize your earning potential through following up.

Let's take a look at just some of the areas where I make sure I provide regular or timely client follow-up.

Retirement Planning

A sixty-one-year-old client tells me that she wants to retire next year when she turns sixty-two. I put it into my Customer Relationship Management (CRM) software to give her a call in six months to discuss if she is still on track to her early-retirement goal. I also put into her file a series of questions to ask when making that call:

What are your current 401(k) balances?

Are your allocations properly aligned?

Are you planning a nonworking or a soft retirement?

Will you be paying off your mortgage or selling your home and cashing out?

Will you be downsizing your lifestyle, either by selling your home or moving to a lower-cost-of-living community?

Are you, or can you become, debt free?

When it is time to make the call, I am ready to have a substantive conversation out of which I can put together a retirement plan that satisfies my client's wants and needs. By the time my client is sixty-two, her retirement plan is in place and she can relax.

Paying off a Car Loan

A client in his mid-thirties says that he has thirteen more car payments at $500 a month. I will put into my calendar to contact him in twelve months to discuss taking that $500 and starting an IRA. This takes what may have been a previous vague discussion about starting an IRA and puts it into a specific action.

Annual Bonuses

Who doesn't like to see large sums of money in their checking accounts? Too often, clients view bonuses as disposable income windfalls rather than opportunities to increase future investments. I reach out to my clients who receive annual bonuses about one month before the bonus payment is due to discuss how *we* can allocate a portion of the bonus to investments (usually 50 percent or more) while still leaving my clients with additional disposable income. In discussing investments, I always use the word *we* to convey that we are a team working together for their financial success.

Tax Law Changes

Tax laws change annually—whether they are the sweeping cuts and reforms that we've seen in 2017 or incremental ones. It's important to stay informed about changes. I've had clients come to me who have been making $166.66-per-month automated investments to their IRAs because when they set up the payment, there was a $2,000-per-year maximum investment. There have been several changes since then, yet they never adjusted for the changes. I always advise clients to talk to an appropriately licensed professional. Clients may determine that they can increase their monthly payments to reflect the current annual maximums.

These are only a few of the many things to think about proactively and follow up with your clients on a timely basis. The more often you reach out to them with moneymaking and money-saving advice, the more indispensable your services become, and the less likely they are to believe that Robo Advisors or other do-it-yourself options are right for them.

Chapter Summary: Simple Ideas for Client Follow-Up

✓ Use CRM software to help manage client follow-up schedules.

✓ Call clients every ninety days, if possible, or every six months at minimum. Use this time to see where the client is currently and what has changed, is changing or soon to change.

✓ Pay attention to what your clients are telling you. Get emotionally invested in their success and move beyond a transactional attitude. Having an emotional investment helps you ask the right questions and make the right decisions.

✓ Use the word *we* instead of *you* to stress that you are a team working together for their financial success.

*The people who tell you not to worry about the little things
have never tried sleeping in a room with a mosquito.*
—Robert E. Farrell, *Give 'Em the
Pickle . . . and they'll be back!*

CHAPTER 8

Common Mistake:
To Get Big, Focus on the Big Things

Simple Idea:
Never Be Too Big to Do the Little Things

Go big or go home. No guts, no glory. Big risks, big rewards. Expressions like these help us build courage to take risks. They are also simple affirmations that reinforce an idea that one should jump from point A to point C to get ahead in life. Who needs point B?

We all do!

To "go big," "get the glory," and yield the "big rewards" takes many small actions along the way. Forgetting the little things is a big deal. I know. I learned that lesson early in my career.

I had the opportunity to spend a day and a half with three other people at the Jersey Shore house of Joe Ensor. For those of you not familiar with the name, Joe was a giant in our field, both physically—he was 6'4" and three hundred pounds—and professionally. He was more than a financial advisor. He was a motivational speaker who spurred his audience to greater heights through presentations like "14 Principles of Success" and "Recruit to Build." It was a great honor for me to be invited to spend time with a man I consider my mentor.

The four of us spent Friday night with Joe for an evening of questions and answers. He told us that on Saturday morning he had invited twenty more people to join us for a breakfast meeting and gathering. He also told us that we four would be doing the cooking for everyone. As someone who had never thought of himself as a competent cook, let alone one who could cook for so many people, it sounded like a daunting task.

Joe was a former restaurateur, so not only was food very important to him, he also knew how to serve a lot of people in a short amount of time. Joe gave each of the four of us food-preparation assignments. I was in charge of toast. I sighed with relief. How hard could making toast be?

Well, Joe had a very specific way he wanted me to prepare the toast. I had to put four pieces of bread in the toaster and when they popped up, I immediately put in another four pieces. While they were toasting I buttered the previous batch. He had a whole production line for toast. It seemed easy enough. I suddenly felt confident in my toast-making skills.

About ten minutes into my duties, the other guests arrived, several of whom I knew. One of them came over and we started talking. I got distracted. The toast got burnt.

A booming voice suddenly filled the room. "Lashner, what did you do to the toast?" I stammered an apology about getting distracted. Joe boomed, "Imagine if I had given you real responsibility," and then walked away.

His point was made. If I didn't see the little things as being important, why should people trust me with the big things?

Consistently taking care of the little things is an important part of working with integrity and honoring your commitments. As financial advisors, our word is like the signature at the bottom of a check—it's either good or it is not. Notice that I used the term *our word* because it is okay if our clients don't follow through. It is not okay if we don't follow through.

Doing the little things may seem tedious—even at times unnecessary—but in my experience little things mean a lot. Use your assistant and/or administrative staff as your follow-up backup system. Consistently show clients how you handle little things and they will build confidence and trust in you to handle bigger things.

CHAPTER SUMMARY:
NEVER BE TOO BIG TO DO THE LITTLE THINGS

- ✓ Forgetting the little things is a big deal.

- ✓ If you don't see the little things as important, why should people trust you with the big things? Remember in Chapter 7 I told you about a client who had a small IRA with me yet didn't consider me when he had a significant investment to make? It was not because he only knew me from handling a small investment; *it was because I didn't do the "little thing" of consistent follow-up.*

- ✓ Our word should be like the signature at the bottom of a check—it's either good or it's not.

- ✓ Let your administrative staff be your backup system and help remind you to take care of the little things.

Politeness is the art of choosing among your thoughts.
—Madame de Stael

CHAPTER 9

Common Mistake:
Bringing Up Politics with Clients

Simple Idea:
Talk Economics, Avoid Politics

*T*HIS IS THE SHORTEST chapter in the book, but equally important as the others. It can also be summed up in one sentence:

DON'T TALK POLITICS WITH CLIENTS!

Even if you know that your client shares your views, they may be sitting there thinking, "I agree, but my brother-in-law sure doesn't. I can't refer him to this advisor."

Remember, referrals are part of your compensation. Why say anything that might negatively impact your income?

What if your client brings up political topics? Turn the conversation to economics and how current laws or policies impact investment options. Just stay clear of political opinions.

> *When you make a mistake, there are only three things you should ever do about it: admit it, learn from it, and don't repeat it.*
> Paul "Bear" Bryant

CHAPTER 10

Common Mistake: Compounding Mistakes by Not Handling Them Properly

Simple Idea: Admit, Learn, Don't Repeat

*E*VERYONE MAKES MISTAKES. To err is human, right? What's important is, What do you do after the mistake has been made? The late, legendary University of Alabama football coach "Bear" Bryant said there are only three things you should do: admit it, learn from it, and don't repeat it. The last thing you want to do is compound the mistake by repeating it, or possibly even worse, ignoring it.

In the previous eight chapters we looked at common mistakes I have seen made by financial advisors—most definitely including myself—and simple ideas to correct or avoid making them. In this chapter we will also look at mistakes that may not have been made by the advisor yet remain the advisor's responsibility to remedy.

In my experience I have found four types of mistakes in the financial industry:

- Advisor's mistakes.
- Client mistakes.

- Mistakes in the system.
- Mistakes that actually don't exist.

Advisor's Mistakes

The majority of this book has been about big-picture mistakes advisors can make and their impact on overall business. Here are two examples of specific mistakes that might be made by an advisor and how to address each one so it doesn't lead to bigger mistakes and consequences.

"Fat Finger" Mistake and Resolution

In filling out a client's application, the advisor presses the wrong key—what I refer to as a "fat finger" mistake—causing the client's mailing address to be off by one number. As careful as people are, occasionally mistakes like this are made. When the client fails to receive the documentation in the expected time frame, he calls the advisor. The advisor tells the client she will look into it. There should never be any defensiveness on the advisor's part.

The advisor investigates and discovers the address had been wrongly entered. The mistake is corrected, and the advisor ensures that the documents will be promptly mailed to the correct address. The client is informed that everything has been corrected and the documents are on their way. The advisor should follow up directly with the client to confirm the documents have been received.

Mistake of Omission

Your client Mike calls with a change that needs to be made; it's not a major change but one that has time constraints. You assure him that you will take care of it. Mike hangs up the phone, confident that you will do as you say. A week goes by and Mike hasn't heard back from you.

He's starting to worry because the deadline is coming up. He grows impatient, and a little angry. Mike calls your office wanting to know why his request hasn't been handled. Your assistant is surprised. She says the change was made a week ago.

The financial advisor took care of Mike's need immediately yet failed to call Mike or empower her assistant to contact clients after each requested action was taken. Mistakes of omission are costly obstacles in providing an outstanding customer experience.

Putting a system in place of giving clients regular updates on all requests is a proven way to keep simple yet costly mistakes from being repeated. Remember: *If it's important to my client, it's important to me.*

CLIENT MISTAKE

Client mistakes can easily happen either by the client's initiative or through the advisor's suggestion clients use websites or toll-free numbers to make seemingly simple changes or transactions.

Here is one not uncommon situation: A client has both a traditional and a Roth IRA, which were set up through their advisor. They are ready to send in a full contribution to their Roth IRA. They decide it's a simple enough transaction that they can handle it via website. No need to "bother" their financial advisor.

By not conferring with their advisor, however, they aren't reminded that, unlike a traditional IRA, they lose up-front tax deductions on their Roth IRA contributions.

When the client ends up owing more than expected to the IRS at the end of the year, they call their financial advisor, upset that they weren't told about Roth IRA deduction impact.

What should an advisor do when a client is upset at him for his or her own mistake? It doesn't matter who made the mistake. All that matters is how it can be rectified. In the case of the Roth IRA, the advisor might perform a financial health check on the client and see how the lost deduction might be offset through other means. The bottom line is to seek a solution that can help satisfy the client. You want the client to associate you with the solution, not the problem. Above all, never get defensive, because nothing good can come from it.

Mistakes in the System

These are rarer occurrences, but sometimes there is lost mail or emails resulting in paperwork not arriving on time or deadlines missed. In my experience mistakes in the system happen more frequently with the federal government than in the private sector. It is especially a problem with Thrift Savings Plans for civil servants and uniformed service members. Again, as with any mistake, do your best to resolve the issue for the client in a timely manner. It helps you build trust and value.

Mistakes That Don't Exist— Except in the Client's Mind

Money is a sensitive and emotional topic for most people. Sometimes a client will speak with a friend who tells her about a moneymaking investment or a money-saving technique and your client confronts you as to why you haven't told her about the investment or technique, completely unaware that the investment or technique might not apply to her or be right for her needs and goals.

Other times, clients misunderstand some information and believe you have made a mistake or are not looking out for their best interests. One area where I have seen this happen is fund rebalancing.

The client has two mutual funds with the same company. One fund is aggressive, the other more conservative. The client's initial investment was split fifty-fifty between the funds. The client does not realize, or has forgotten, that the funds are being automatically rebalanced. When the aggressive fund has risen, money is taken out and put back into the

10 COMMON MISTAKES FINANCIAL ADVISORS MAKE

conservative fund so that the balance remains fifty-fifty. Or, conversely, if the conservative fund has grown slightly, while the aggressive fund has declined, money is taken from the conservative fund and put into the aggressive one. In either case, the client sees the quarterly report with changes and calls the advisor wanting to know why shares are being sold and worried about nonexistent fees. The advisor explains about automatic rebalancing.

Reaching out to clients every ninety days to address any concerns, questions or issues is an effective way to ease clients' minds and offset the types of "mistakes" that don't exist.

Throughout this book we have taken a look at several customer-service issues and problems. I've chosen these examples purposely because it is very likely that every one of us has experienced frustrating customer-service calls. But there is another reason I have focused on customer-service issues: As financial advisors, we are in a service business, and it is imperative that we put our clients first. This is especially true in how we handle mistakes.

Here is one last customer-service story that demonstrates the dangers of compounding mistakes.

About one year ago, I received a welcome letter from a telephone company saying that I had purchased two iPhones in a state that is on the other side of the country from where I live. I immediately saw this as likely identity theft; somebody had purchased the phones in my name. Concerned, I wanted to call the company. I looked at the letter several times before I found the toll-free number. I called and was immediately confronted with menu options. Nothing matched with fraud; everything was about being an existing customer or adding services.

After almost twenty minutes of growing frustration, a representative answered. I started telling him about my fraud concerns, but was interrupted and told I had the wrong department. He offered to transfer me to the right one. I returned to hold, for another ten minutes. I again started to explain the situation, and was again told I was speaking to the wrong department. She said she would transfer me, but instead, I was disconnected.

Now, with rising anger, I started the process over again. This time I reached the right department—but it had taken over an hour of my time to get there. I explained the situation to the representative, who assured me the company would credit the account for the $280 I had been billed. I said fine and thought everything was settled.

Two weeks later, I received a bill for $280. Perhaps the credit and the bill had crossed in the mail. I wasn't going to risk not doing anything, however, so once again I started the process of reaching the right department. I told the representative about the situation and that it should all be in the notes. The representative said there is no record of it. Once again, I repeated all of the information.

I waited two weeks, then called back to verify that everything had been taken care of. It had not yet been completed, but at least this time they did have all the information recorded. Rather than calling back once again to verify, I asked if they could send email verification that I have been credited and the bogus account closed. The representative said he would send the email after we hang up.

Needless to say, I never received the email. After another week I called once again and spoke to a different person. She assured me the account had been credited and closed.

Five separate phone calls—plus two wrong transfers and a disconnect—and several hours of my time were spent resolving a mistake that I had not made. Clearly, I was not the first person this situation happened to. The company should have a fraud resolution system in place designed to keep their customers happy.

This was a company I wasn't doing business with in the first place, and after experiencing the way they handled this mistake, I would never consider doing business with them. Not only wouldn't I do business with them, I told my friends and family about this frustrating experience. Perhaps their buying habits have been influenced by my story. Multiply that by the hundreds, thousands of people that have gone through similar experiences over the years and you can see how little things, like having a system in place when there is a problem, can have a big impact.

The lesson I learned from my experience was to view a mistake as an opportunity to solve client issues in a way that reassures them and takes the responsibility off their shoulders. Build client confidence that you will resolve issues simply and efficiently. That is how we build trusted, long-term relationships. That is how we create Raving Fans.

CHAPTER SUMMARY:
ADMIT, LEARN, DON'T REPEAT MISTAKES

- ✓ There are only three things you should do after a mistake: Admit it, learn from it, and don't repeat it.

- ✓ There are four types of mistakes: advisor's mistakes, client mistakes, mistakes in the system and mistakes that actually don't exist.

- ✓ Mistakes of omission are costly obstacles to providing an outstanding customer experience.

- ✓ It doesn't matter who made the mistake. All that matters is how you can rectify it. You want the client to associate you with the solution, not the problem.

- ✓ Never get defensive about mistakes.

- ✓ View mistakes as an opportunity to solve client issues in a way that reassures them and takes the responsibility off their shoulders.

- ✓ Build client confidence that you will resolve issues simply and efficiently: That is how we build trusted, long-term relationships; that is how we create Raving Fans.

> *Things work out best for those who make
> the best of how things work out.*
> —John Wooden

A Few Thoughts to Close

THE TEN MISTAKES FINANCIAL advisors make that are highlighted in this book were chosen not only because they are common across the industry, but also because there are simple ideas and best practices that can be put into place to eliminate or avoid them, and to turn them into opportunities. I hope that you have found the ideas presented thought provoking and that you will incorporate the appropriate simple ideas and best-practice actions into your business.

As financial advisors, it is important that we let go of the idea that we are selling products and programs and embrace the idea that we are selling a client experience based on trust. The more that technology and automation take over areas of our business, as they have in other areas of our life, the more essential it is that we are there to provide the necessary human contact that can adjust to their needs, alleviate their concerns, and see their financial world through their eyes in ways algorithms can never be programmed to do.

However, as the customer-service stories throughout this book clearly demonstrate, just because clients can speak to another person does not mean that person is properly trained and equipped to handle mistakes and issues. Not only do you, as the financial advisor, need to stay up to date and informed on the industry and on your individual clients' financial health, you need to have an assistant and/or administrative staff capable of professionally handling client relations. Having a staff—even if it is only a staff of one—makes it easy to develop and implement a systematic client follow-up process, which goes a long way in developing happy clients. You might not think you can afford to hire a staff, but I can assure you it is much costlier to try to run your entire business on your own.

When you place the client's concerns first and establish a relationship of trust, you have made yourself referable. I strongly believe that prequalified referrals and introductions are the lifeblood to a successful business. But remember to be patient in your expectations of receiving client referrals—the best referrals often come years down the road.

As you read this book, I hope it will open your mind to a new mind-set of creating a personalized experience for your clients. Mine is based on delivering peace of mind. Think about what your experience would be. Incorporate these simple ideas and put your experience into action.

Finally, I'll leave you with what has become my mantra to creating happy, loyal clients: Take care of your clients or somebody else will.

❖

Acknowledgments

This book would not have been possible without the contributions of the late Ronnie Scholl, my first assistant, who was indispensable to me and my family, both personally and professionally; and Christina Ridgeway, who stepped into Ronnie's big shoes and created a legacy of her own. She has become vital to me in all areas of my business. Most important, I want to thank my wife, Maria, and my children, Jacob and Allie—they inspire me to be the best I can be. I hope I make them proud.

About the Author

Howard Lashner has more than thirty years' experience serving clients in the financial services industry. Throughout his long and tenured career, Howard has served as a sounding board for his clients, earning their trust and confidence with his long-term commitment to helping them achieve their goals. Howard prides himself on helping his clients get on the path to achieving financial independence.

Howard frequently speaks to large audiences of financial advisors across the United States and Canada on topics that include the importance of a client-focused business.

To contact Howard directly:
Howard@lashner.biz
(267) 784-4420

Made in the USA
Columbia, SC
21 January 2019